WHY NOT ME?

Also by Al Franken

RUSH LIMBAUGH IS A BIG FAT IDIOT
AND OTHER OBSERVATIONS

I'M GOOD ENOUGH, I'M SMART ENOUGH,
AND DOGGONE IT, PEOPLE LIKE ME!

WHY NOT ME?

THE INSIDE STORY
OF THE MAKING
AND UNMAKING
OF THE
FRANKEN PRESIDENCY

AL FRANKEN

DELACORTE PRESS

Published by
Delacorte Press
Random House, Inc.
1540 Broadway
New York, New York 10036

Interior photography and digital illustrations by Paul D'Innocenzo ©1998
Backgrounds of photos on pages 189 and 195 courtesy of Corbis.
Cartoon illustration on page 76 by John Jonik

LIBRARY OF CONGRESS CATALOGING-IN-PUBLICATION DATA
Franken, Al.
    Why not me? : the inside story of the making and unmaking
of the Franken presidency / Al Franken.
        p.   cm.
    ISBN 0-385-31809-X
    I. Title.
    PN6162.F717   1999
    813'.54—dc21   98-43979
                                                        CIP

Manufactured in the United States of America
Published simultaneously in Canada

January 1999

10 9 8 7 6 5 4 3 2 1

TO BILLY KIMBALL,
without whose constant encouragement
this book could not have been written

DISCLAIMER

I have been asked by the lawyer for my publisher, Delacorte Press, to begin this book with a disclaimer.

Some background: The last decade has seen an explosion in civil litigation of all types, not the least of which are suits for libel and defamation of character. Though these lawsuits almost invariably fail, they can be costly in both time and money for the defendant, who in this case would be me and Delacorte Press. As a strong believer in the First Amendment, I would consider it a privilege to defend my constitutional rights in court, but Delacorte evidently feels otherwise.

Delacorte has suggested some specific language that, despite repeated efforts, I have found impossible to improve upon.

1. "This book is a work of satire and is thereby entitled to the same protection afforded Larry Flynt when he published an ad parody for Campari in which evangelist Jerry Falwell described losing his virginity during an incestuous encounter with his mother in an outdoor toilet."

2. "Even though this book contains many names of real people, (such as President Bill Clinton, Chief Justice William Rehnquist, and former *Grizzly Adams* star Dan Haggerty), and real corporations (such as Archer Daniels Midland Company and the Chiquita banana company), nothing depicted in the book (such as my attempt to assassinate Saddam Hussein) actually happened."

3. "No insurance company (Aetna, Prudential, etc.) has engaged in the acts depicted (illegal campaign contributions, money laundering, etc.), and I have no factual basis to believe that, in general, the insurance industry is any more or less corrupt than any other large American industry, such as the music business or publishing."

4. "Please note that the earlier statements that 'this book is a work of satire' and that 'nothing depicted in the book . . . actually happened' also apply to the 'letters on letterhead,' which are every bit as 'fictional' as the rest of the book. While not exactly 'fictional,' the newspaper and magazine mastheads are 'fake' and their use is 'unauthorized.'"

5. "The book contains manipulated photos, including the one on the cover of me being sworn in as president with Bill and Hillary Clinton and Chief Justice William Rehnquist looking on in horror."

6. "Neither I nor Delacorte can be held responsible for any injuries that might occur as a result of the use of this book for any purpose for which it is not intended, such as hitting a mouse or propping up a car axle while changing a tire."

WHY NOT ME?

AL FRANKEN

November 12, 1998

Dear Chief Justice Rehnquist,

First let me say that I am a big fan of your work as a Justice of the United States Supreme Court, and your term as Chief Justice in particular. I have closely followed many of your decisions, particularly those involving the tax deductibility of a writer's home office. I often tell people who compliment me on my previous book *Rush Limbaugh Is a Big Fat Idiot* that they have Chief Justice Rehnquist to thank, because it would probably never have been written if not for your wise decisions regarding writers' home offices. Thank you.

Now to the matter at hand. For my next book, *Why Not Me?*, I have decided to take a humorous look at my campaign for president of the United States and my subsequent one hundred and forty-four days in office. Being an intelligent man, you will grasp immediately that this is make-believe and is intended as a joke. As you know, I have not been elected president, and I have no plans to run for office—local, regional, or national.

The current concept for the cover, which I think you'll agree is a funny one, is of a mock "swearing-in" featuring onlookers who are clearly apprehensive about the prospects of a Franken Administration. (You see, I probably wouldn't be a good president. That's why the onlookers would be apprehensive.) Anyway, the good people at Delacorte, my publisher, have asked me to recruit as many real people as possible to participate in the cover shoot. So far, we have tentative yeses from Dick Cavett, "Weird" Al Yankovic, and former president Gerald Ford.

We would be willing to work around the Court's docket and travel to Washington if necessary. However, it would certainly be more convenient for us if you could come to New York for the shoot. We would be willing to reimburse you for off-peak train fare. Our travel agent, Julian at Liberty Travel, who is very good, suggests you call 1-800-USA-RAIL for train schedules and reservations, and to determine when the off-peak fares are in effect.

AL FRANKEN

If for some reason you are unable to meet our current deadline for the shoot, which is this coming Tuesday, I am wondering: In your opinion as a lawyer and Supreme Court Justice, is it legal to use a photograph of a person doing something very specific (such as swearing in a president) without that person's permission? If possible, could you give me an answer on this by next Tuesday? Also, do you have any old photographs of yourself swearing in a president, such as Clinton? In particular, do you have any shots where you look apprehensive, nervous, uncomfortable, or angry?

Thank you in advance for your assistance.

Sincerely yours,

Al Franken

Al Franken

November 14, 1998

Dear Mr. Franken,

A wise man once said that no one ever got anywhere in this world without learning how to read upside down. I was reminded of this recently while standing in Chief Justice Rehnquist's chambers awaiting his instructions on how to vote on a complex antitrust matter. I happened to notice your letter on his desk, sitting upside down (from my point of view) and apparently unread by the Chief Justice. Knowing Chief Justice Rehnquist as I do, I can tell you that it is most unlikely that he will accede to your request.

Unfortunately, unlike David Souter—who enjoys jokes of all sorts, particularly puns—Chief Justice Rehnquist has virtually no sense of humor (although he did enjoy the "Dorf on Torts" video that Archer Daniels Midland sent to all of us at Christmas).

In contrast, I myself have an excellent sense of humor, and have often been complimented on my stock of after-dinner jokes, both ribald and not. Therefore, I humbly offer my services as a substitute for Chief Justice Rehnquist, who I repeat is not funny like I am. I might add that there is no constitutional prohibition against an Associate Justice swearing in a new president, or so Justice Scalia tells me. I have enclosed a series of photographs of myself with different facial expressions, running the gamut from sad to happy, which my wife thinks you might find useful in designing your cover. She also said to tell you that I have my own robes and Bible and that, if necessary, I could probably borrow a Torah from Justice Ginsburg.

I could be available at your convenience at any time or place. I should add that I currently have 33,000 frequent flyer miles on United and 17,000 on Delta.

I will be calling you in a few days to discuss this matter further. Thank you in advance for your consideration.

Hopefully yours,

Clarence Thomas

Clarence Thomas

P.S. Justice Souter thinks it might be funny if I were standing in my underpants as a play on "legal briefs." What do you think?

AL FRANKEN

November 19, 1998

Dear Justice Thomas,

I was surprised and delighted to receive your letter of November 14th.
Although I very much appreciate the time and trouble you took to write,
as well as the "happy-sad" photos, I regret to inform you that we will not
be able to use you on the cover of *Why Not Me?* Let me explain. I am
intending to take the high road in my book by avoiding any cheap humor
and hackneyed references. It is my opinion, and that of virtually everyone
I spoke to, that having you on the cover would fall into both categories.

While you may believe that you have not been the butt of jokes since the
whole "Coke can" business during your confirmation hearings, I can assure
you that within the humor fraternity you are still considered a very easy
target. For your information, a large majority of the jokes focus on your
notorious obsession with pornography, while a small minority are
devoted to your complete lack of qualifications for the High Court.

In conclusion, thank you again for your interest in *Why Not Me?*
and permit me to wish you the best of luck with your future projects.

Sincerely yours,

(Dictated but not signed)

Al Franken

P.S. If you have Long Dong Silver's phone number, please call my assistant,
Geoff. We are thinking of having Long Dong pose in drag on the cover as
my wife.

December 12, 1998

Dear Mr. Franken,

Chief Justice Rehnquist has asked me to respond to your recent letter to say, first of all, no; and, second of all, to ask you how we might get in touch with Tim Conway. The Chief Justice also told me to tell you that since he is a public figure, your right to use his likeness on the cover is protected by the First Amendment as long as the photo in question is clearly intended for humorous effect.

A previous court's decision in the matter of *Falwell* v. *Flynt* is regarded as a binding precedent, though the Chief Justice wishes me to add as a personal request that you not depict him engaging in sexual intercourse with his mother in an outhouse.

Furthermore, he suggests that as an alternative you might wish to consider Justice Thomas for your cover, since there is no constitutional prohibition against an Associate Justice administering the Oath of Office to an incoming president.

Thank you very much for your interest in Chief Justice Rehnquist, and please don't hesitate to contact us again if you locate Tim Conway's number.

Sincerely yours,

(DICTATED BUT NOT SIGNED)

Michael Saperstein

Clerk to the Chief Justice
of the United States Supreme Court

PART ONE

THE
AUTHORIZED
CAMPAIGN
AUTOBIOGRAPHY

DARING TO LEAD

"Mandatory reading
for all Americans
who care about the
future of their country."
—**Norman J. Ornstein**
*American Enterprise
Institute*

AL FRANKEN

WITH TONY SCHWARTZ

CHAPTER ONE

THE COURAGE TO DARE

The Pulitzer Prize–winning journalist David Broder once wrote something to the effect that "anyone who's willing to do what it takes to be president should be immediately disqualified." And that's why I want to be your president.

As a regular voter for most of my adult life, I have grown to share the average American's disgust with "politics as usual."

Year after year, election after election, we've seen candidates prostitute themselves on the altar of special interests: corporate fat cats, six-figure lobbyists in Italian loafers, women, gays, and the so-called disadvantaged. Is it any wonder that with each passing election we've witnessed lower and lower voter turnout as the public's skepticism turns to cynicism, which leads to apathy and despair, which can cause sleeplessness, dry-mouth, and loss of sex drive? And that's why I want to be your president.

The reason I'm running is very simple: to restore America's lost faith in its leaders. Of course, the high-paid media pundits may say this claim is grandiose, that I'm not qualified, that I'm deluded or even seriously mentally ill.

But I think the American people know better.

Yes, I know the job of President of the United States can be a difficult one. Full of challenges, decisions, and meetings. Furthermore, a president must be diplomatic and statesmanlike, which sometimes can mean being nice to people he doesn't like. As the leader of the world's only remaining superpower, the President can ignite nuclear Armageddon at the touch of a button, killing billions. That is a responsibility not to be taken lightly.

Yes, the President does earn two hundred thousand dollars a year. But when you break that down on an hourly basis, it's no more than a union plumber in the New York City public school system or a third-rate heart surgeon, neither of whom confronts life and death decisions on a daily basis, except the heart surgeon. Still, by the standards of the forgotten middle class, the working poor, and the not-working poor, two hundred thousand dollars is a nice chunk of change. But, unlike some of the candidates I'll be running against, for me the money is secondary.

I recognize that any president necessarily stands on the shoulders of giants: Washington, Lincoln, etc. Anyone running for president must wrestle with the nagging suspicion that he somehow doesn't "measure up" to Washington and Lincoln and the others. But self-doubt is a luxury, and anyone who knows Al Franken knows that he selects his luxuries very, very carefully. And that's why I want to be your president.

My inspiration to run for president is threefold. First, there is the Franken family tradition of public service, which began back in the old country when my uncle Moishe left his little village in Russia. Everyone in the village said it was a public service. But seriously, this is not a time to indulge in traditional Yiddish humor. Or so my media advisors tell me.

Second, as a parent, every day I look into the eyes of my children, not only to make sure that they're not on drugs (they're not, thank God) but also to remind myself of the legacy I will leave behind. As Miss America 1988, Kaye Lani Rae Rafko, once said, "Our children are America's future." I agree. And I have made a solemn pledge to my children that I will leave this planet in at least as good a condition as I found it—if not better.

Third, I have been inspired by the example of some recent candidates for our nation's highest office: former Tennessee governor Lamar Alexander, eccentric businessman Ross Perot, Reagan-era functionary Alan Keyes, and tire king Morry Taylor. When I looked at them I said to myself, "Hey, I can do that!" The decision to run for president is not one that is made casually. I am well aware of the toll this will take on my family and on Colin Powell, who will never hear the end of it if I win.

Furthermore, campaigning for president can be a full-time job, leaving very little time for making money by developing concepts for sitcoms, let alone writing entire scripts. Nevertheless, both I and my therapist believe that I am fully prepared for the task that lies ahead, physically, mentally, and emotionally, as long as I keep up with our regular Tuesday and Thursday sessions and group on Saturday.

But the decision was not mine and my therapist's alone. There was a third person involved. The most important person in my life. Franni Franken is not just my wife, not just the mother of my children, not just the woman who cleans my house—she's also my best friend. By that I mean we have sex together. But after the sex, we often have a conversation. That's what makes us not just friends but best friends. This is not to say that if you and your spouse are not friends, that you shouldn't vote for me. Because I know what that's like too. God knows, we've had our problems. When I told Franni that I was going to run for president, she said, "Fine. If that'll make you happy." That's the kind of woman she is. So, she's on board.

My children, on the other hand, were another matter. Both Joe and Thomasin felt that as members of the First Family they would be living under a microscope with no privacy whatsoever; that the twenty-four-hour-a-day news cycle and modern, sophisticated electronic news-gathering techniques would afford them no opportunity to grow up in anything resembling a normal household. My teenage daughter, Thomasin, who is just getting her feet wet in the dating "scene," whined that trusting her private life in these delicate years to the pledged word and promised restraint of the nation's bottom-line-obsessed, cutthroat news media was no better than leaving a starving fox to guard a fully stocked henhouse. Her little brother, Joe, added that no matter how much they would try, his peers at school could not help but treat him differently if he were the son of the President and that he feared losing the companionship of close friends during this crucial formative period and even his very innocence itself.

Kids!

In our family we make important decisions by consensus. Everyone—Franni, Joe, Thomasin, and myself—must agree before we embark upon major life changes. (That's why we never bought that DeLorean I wanted.) It was time for a family meeting.

On a rainy Sunday afternoon in March our family gathered around the kitchen table, as so many other American families do, whether to cope with a family crisis, tell a joke, watch a sporting event, play cards, discuss a string of unsolved rapes in the neighborhood, or just have a snack.

While my advisors waited anxiously in the next room, I laid out the pros and cons of a campaign for the presidency and shared my vision for America's future with my family. I described for my kids an America where every child, not just the children of the privileged few, would have clean water, access to the Internet, and regular vaccinations.

"You're just pulling this stuff out of your ass to make us feel guilty," Thomasin said. "I didn't ask to be inoculated."

Franni came in on my side like a true champion. "Thomasin! If your dad's going to be president, you won't be able to use words like *ass* at the dinner table."

"My point exactly," Thomasin replied.

"And if your dad is president, you won't be able to answer back either," Franni riposted.

"Right," Thomasin said, rolling her eyes. "Mom, you're not doing yourself any good here."

Sensing the wisdom of her daughter's words, Franni decided to change tack and snuck me a conspiratorial look that seemed to say "You catch more flies with honey than you do with vinegar."

"Honey, you know how important being president is to your dad. And I'm sure he understands how much you dislike the idea of his being president. But this is something he wants us to agree on as a family. So, what if Dad took us all to Hawaii for spring vacation? You'd feel better about Dad running for president then, wouldn't you?"

Franni was on to something. Because she spends so much more time with the children than I do, she knew how much a simple ten-thousand-dollar vacation to Hawaii would mean to a status-seeking Manhattan teenager. But it was my son, Joe, who provided the clincher.

"Thomasin, let's just take the trip. A.) He'll never win. And B.) *The Simpsons* is on."

And so, a month later, jet-lagged, tanned, and with my family firmly behind me, I began my quest to lead the world, trusting in God to show me the way.

CHAPTER TWO
THE JOURNEY BEGINS

My dad, Herman Franken, used to say that if you want to know where a man stands, you've got to know how he got to where he's standing. Dad wasn't so good with words, but I think you can see what he was driving at.

I was born in a nondescript ranch house, the son of the son of immigrants and the son of a daughter of a son and daughter of immigrants.

We lived in a little town called Christhaven, Minnesota. We were the only Jews for miles. My father owned and ran Franken's Department Store, which by the time I was born had only three departments: lawn furniture, men's work clothes, and driveway sealants. Modern inventory techniques had not yet made their way to Christhaven.

Dad instilled in me the values of hard work and thrift. I always used to tell him that if he fired some of his lazy and slow-witted employees, who frankly had very little to do anyway, that he wouldn't have to work so hard or be so thrifty. But he also believed in loyalty. Also, he said that the Gentiles brought in business.

In addition to loyalty, hard work, and thrift, Dad felt that trust—even when it meant extending credit to our deadbeat neighbors—was important, although I realized early on what Dad seemed not to: that trust would only lead to more hard work and thriftiness.

Dad also believed in the innate goodness of human nature, and that everyone deserved a second chance. One of my earliest memories of my father is him giving a youthful shoplifter a stern lecture and then a free candy bar instead of calling the police. Perhaps that's why Franken's was so popular with Christhaven's many shoplifters.

Ironically, when his business finally went under, after the store had been foreclosed on by the bank and our assets attached by Dad's creditors, leaving us with nothing but a mountain of unpaid bills, no one gave Dad a second chance. Always a proud man, convinced that Franken's would soon reopen with more departments than ever, Dad refused to declare bankruptcy, leading to the first of several short jail terms.

I don't know exactly when Dad started to become bitter and disillusioned, but I think it might have been in jail. Because when he returned from his second stretch in prison, Dad seemed not to be motivated by hard work, thriftiness, loyalty, trust, or innate faith in human goodness so much anymore. He seemed to be motivated by revenge.

Dad sued the town for the very first time when I was just eleven.

It was Christmastime. Dad had never mentioned to me how much Christhaven's lavish Nativity display in the town square had bothered him. But judging by the vehemence with which he now began to attack it in court, it must have stuck in his craw for quite some time. Working with an ACLU lawyer he had met while serving time, Dad sued the town, demanding that it either dismantle the manger scene or erect an equally magnificent menorah.

I'll never forget the sight of the wrecking ball knocking the heads off the Three Kings while my dad merrily waved the court order under the mayor's nose. It was then that I realized what one man with a good lawyer can accomplish.

While Dad seemed to have found a new lust for life, his new hobby—suing the town—was not one the whole family could enjoy. In fact, we think that my brother Otto's drinking problem and sex addiction can be traced back to some of the difficulties that he and I encountered in school as the result of my father's notoriety. My mother still weeps when she recounts the story of how Otto and I came home from school one day, swastikas drawn on our foreheads with blue Magic Markers.

There was no mistaking it. This was anti-Semitism. It was as plain as the swastika on my forehead.

It's hard to imagine now, but in 1962 many people felt that only members of certain religious groups, such as Presbyterians and Episcopalians, for example, were qualified to be president. In fact, America had just elected (and was about to shoot) its first Catholic president. In 1960, when John F. Kennedy launched his bid for the White House, there were many, my parents among them, who believed that a Catholic was unfit to serve as America's leader; that all Catholics were in thrall to their puppet master in Rome: the Pope; that they were intellectually ill-equipped for anything more than brutish manual labor and the hollow re-creation of excessive devotion to the superstitious hocus-pocus of their beloved Mother Church.

Irish Catholics in particular were regarded as drunkards and loutish potato eaters who, given half a chance, would sooner spend their last dime in the neighborhood saloon than buy food for their drooling simpleton of a wife and her innumerable brood of squalling infants, each one an unwelcome addition to the Pope's legions of brainless drones.

That was then.

Now, in 1999, only Arabs are held in the sort of contempt once reserved for Catholics, Jews, and Communists. It will still be many years before America has its first Arab president but I hope I am alive to see that day. Also, I think it will be a long time before we see a Hispanic president. Also, blacks.

As it turned out, President Kennedy was one of our greatest and most noble leaders who imbued the office of the presidency with a single-minded devotion to only the loftiest of ideals for the betterment of both our nation and the world. His heroic example and irreproachable moral standing still inspire us today every time we look at a half dollar (the heads side).

But standing there in front of the mirror in 1962, I didn't know much about that. I only knew that I was a little boy with a backward swastika drawn on my head. And I knew one more thing: I knew that prejudice, no matter what form it takes, is bad.

As I scrubbed my forehead, first with soap and water and then with an acetone-based cleaning fluid, I swore that day on the grave of my father, yet to be dug, that I would not let small-minded bigotry or widespread prejudice stop me from fulfilling my destiny. I wouldn't restrict my sights to the traditional "Jewish" professions of medicine, law, accounting, and dentistry. I would make my mark in a sphere of endeavor previously regarded as "off-limits" to my people: show business.

At that time, the number of successful Jews in the performing arts could be counted on one hand: Irving Berlin, Jerry Lewis, Kirk Douglas, Charlie Chaplin, George Gershwin, Ira Gershwin, Eddie Fisher, and Elizabeth Taylor. That was it. Eight Jews. Plus, four of the six Three Stooges. Also, Yitzhak Perlman, but this was years before he acknowledged he was Jewish.

Where am I? Oh yes. Anti-Semitism. It is a scourge that has been with us for centuries, this century being particularly bad. And that's why I want to be your president.

Don't get me wrong. As the first Jewish president of the United States, I am not going to be president of the Jews. I am going to be president for all Americans, Jews and anti-Semites alike. But even before I've signed my first bill or held my first cabinet meeting or given my first order to the joint chiefs of staff, I will have accomplished something very important for our nation. I will have demolished a stereotype: that a Jew lacks what it takes to be president. That we're too insecure, too guilt-ridden, too obsessed with food and eating. All the lies that have been used to oppress us ever since we made the mistake of killing Jesus Christ.

Battling anti-Semitism in all its forms, whether it be manger scenes or movie theaters that stayed open after sundown on Friday night, was the legacy of Herman Franken. It was a legacy I was to inherit prematurely when Dad was killed by an overdose of nitrous oxide while getting a deep cleaning well below the gumline from Dr. Knutsen, a Gentile dentist. It was small comfort that my father, never a happy man, had probably died laughing. Ironically, Dad's notoriety as a litigant brought his family financial security only after his death. Mom didn't even have to threaten to sue. Representatives from Dr. Knutsen's insurance company were there at the funeral with a large ceremonial check.

While some saw simply a large ceremonial check, I saw a magic carpet that would whisk me eastward and somewhat southward to Harvard, made famous in the film *Love Story* and later in *Good Will Hunting*. It was at

Harvard that I would first mingle with our country's "best and brightest" and learn from them what it meant to be both "best" and "brightest" during one of America's "worst" and "darkest" times.

CHAPTER THREE

DAYS OF DECISION

I arrived in Cambridge, Massachusetts, in the fall of 1969, with a suitcase full of clothes and heart full of hope. Mostly, I hoped I wouldn't go to Vietnam.

It's not that I took issue with the courage and honor of our brave men fighting in the jungles of Southeast Asia eleven thousand miles from my dorm. But I had begun to question the wisdom of our leaders after events like the Tet Offensive, the mining of Haiphong Harbor, and the receipt of a letter from my local draft board.

There are many ways for a young man to serve his country. Being drafted into the military is one way. But I learned about another way from my new friends at Harvard, the children of America's power elite, particularly my roommate, Cabot Stanton Hollingshead IV. Early in our collegiate careers Cabot guaranteed his standing as a "Big Man on Campus" by building what was, at the time, Harvard's largest bong. Our two-room suite in Hollingshead Hall became a Mecca for late-night bull sessions during which we, America's future leaders, would "hash" out the "burning" issues of the day. If you know what I'm saying.

Our circle of friends was divided into two camps. The first felt that it was our moral obligation to fight the imperialist aggression of America's racist military-industrial establishment by any means necessary, even if it meant avoiding the draft. The second group just didn't want to die.

I could see the validity of both arguments. And I availed myself of every opportunity to protest the war. In retrospect, the manner in which we protested was not always constructive or mature. For example, there was the time Cabot and I freed all the animals in the Boston Zoo while high on some killer weed we got from his cousin Hollingshead Stanton Cabot VI, now Senator Cabot (R-Tx.).

However, in fairness to Cabot and myself, the photograph of a little girl running naked down Newberry Street while being chased by a galloping giraffe and the picture of an orangutan being executed with a single pistol shot to the head by Boston's chief of police remain two of the most indelible and searing images of that tumultuous era, and undoubtedly served to shorten the war.

In light of the fact that my responsibilities as a student prevented me from serving in the military, some may wonder whether, as president, I would have the moral authority to send our troops, gay or straight, into harm's way. The answer: an emphatic yes.

First of all, if our choice of commander-in-chief were limited to only those who served in the military, we would have to pick from the ranks of dubiously qualified presidential wannabes like John McCain, Bob Kerrey, and Colin Powell.

As for the myth that someone who has not experienced the horrors of war firsthand would be all too eager to send our young men into battle at the drop of a hat, I say that while that might apply to some people, like Newt Gingrich, it wouldn't be true in my case. As for the opposite argument, that someone who has not worn our uniform would be too insecure to put our brave young men and women at risk to defend our vital national interests, all I can say is don't worry about that.

CHAPTER FOUR

MORE DAYS OF DECISION

While my freshman and sophomore years were about drugs, the draft, and deepening paranoia, my junior year brought the first flowering of an entrepreneurial instinct that would ultimately propel me to a career in writing television comedy. In our off-campus commune on Cabot Street, my roommate, Cabot, and I founded the Fabulous Freaky Freakout Company, Inc., and its wholly owned subsidary, the Smoking Doobie Banana Brothers, Ltd., which would offer an eager public such desperately needed products as Mr. Natural T-shirts, Turkish cigarette-rolling machines, and refrigerator magnets with witty slogans. While Cabot busied himself with the art direction, I toiled in the realm of ideas as our wordsmith, dreaming up such phrases as "Still Smokin'," "Keep on Truckin'," and "You've Obviously Mistaken Me for Someone Who Gives a Shit."

Our novelty business seemed to explode overnight. But with success came responsibility. Unlike some candidates who have spent their entire lives moving from one public office to another, such as "judge" or "vice president," I know what it means to meet a payroll. Every other Tuesday, the staff of the Fabulous Freaky Freakout Company—Crazy Momma, Lady J, Trash Can, and Little Biggie—would gather on our beanbag sofa while Cabot and I divided up our profits and distributed each person's share, either in cash or in kind. It was also at this time that I learned first-hand about vital concepts of civil liberties, such as probable cause, search and seizure, and Trash Can's Miranda rights.

As we expanded our product line to include bumper stickers ("If This Van's Rockin' Don't Bother Knockin'"), posters (the one of the baby with the spaghetti on his head), and health products (desensitizing creams, Spanish Fly, and the Acc-U-Jac), I was confronted with the intricacies of the tax code and the inherent impossibility of 100 percent compliance with it.

The lessons of those heady days with the Fabulous Freaky Freakout Company are with me still—lessons about growing a business, building a team of highly motivated professionals, and coping with nit-picking government bureaucracies that refuse to recognize the crucial distinction between an innocent mistake and a deliberate violation. I remember swearing to myself and Crazy Momma, the day they took Little Biggie away for spitting on an IRS auditor who had knocked over his water pipe, that if I were ever in a position to do so I would fight for a system more responsive to the needs of ordinary people, even ordinary people with poor impulse control.

Any president, be it of the United States or of a small novelty company, must learn to be both a leader and a manager. Over time, Cabot and I developed very different management styles. While I devoted more and more of my hours to bringing our business into at least partial compliance with the tax code, Cabot could invariably be found in our basement photography studio, dumping various foods over babies' heads in a fruitless quest to produce a sequel to the poster that had made him a boy wonder in the novelty world.

Looking back, I should have seen the warning signs that Cabot was becoming increasingly unstable. That's another thing a good president must do: beware of mentally unbalanced colleagues. Various factors contributed to Cabot's growing eccentricity: the challenge of balancing his workload and his course load; the disapproval of his father, Governor Hollingshead; and a life-threatening episode involving the potentially deadly interaction between a tab of bad acid and a nonprescription cold medicine.

In retrospect, I should have questioned Cabot's judgment when he insisted that we pour all of the profits from our wildly successful "Hey, Fat Ass!" refrigerator magnet into a new line of posters featuring a baby having corned beef and cabbage dumped over his head. Unfortunately, in the novelty business, as in international diplomacy, timing is everything. The market for posters of babies with food on their heads was saturated. And when Cabot came up with his next idea, a baby with chocolate pudding dumped over his head, I knew that, had we ever managed to incorporate, the time would have come to file for bankruptcy.

Miraculously, a mysterious flash fire turned out to be a blessing in disguise when it destroyed not only the records we never bothered to keep but also our horrible house. Thanks to Governor Hollingshead's comprehensive insurance policy, we received a handsome settlement worth quite a bit more than the silk screens, the boxes of tie-dyed T-shirts, the crate of Afro-picks, and Little Biggie, all of which were consumed in the conflagration.

Cabot, who never fully recovered from the collapse of the Fabulous Freaky Freakout Company, spent the summer traveling with Ken Kesey and the Merry Pranksters and participating in several acid tests. By the time he returned in the fall, he had developed a morbid fear of certain kinds of trees and spent the better part of our senior year hiding in the closets of our rooms at Stanton House. Drugs had claimed another promising young life, at least for the time being. I've often wondered if Cabot's early experience as a drug user and seller played any role in shaping the political philosophy that would propel him to the statehouse and thence to Congress: mandatory death sentences for casual users of illegal drugs. If Cabot's own policies had been law during our years at Harvard, he himself would have been executed time and time again.

CHAPTER FIVE
WATCH OUT, WORLD!

Fresh out of Harvard, with a newly minted sheepskin in hand, I set out into the real world. I planned to embrace the nine-to-five life and merge my spirit with that great mass of humanity, my fellow Americans. I resolved to put my nose to the grindstone, working day-in and day-out to put a roof over my head, feed my family, and pay my taxes. However, after a brief discussion with someone who actually worked in an office, I decided that the real world was not for me.

Instead, I chose a field in which a man's spirit was free to soar and in which he could work very odd hours, or sometimes not come to work at all. Show business.

By the early seventies, the dam had finally broken and Jews were no longer restricted to a few token positions in the entertainment industry, such as being head of Metro Goldwyn Mayer or Warner Bros. And even traditionally WASP bastions like comedy were slowly admitting a trickle of Catholics and Jews. I decided to be a part of this trickle.

Spearheading the campaign to bring Jewish comedy to the mass audience of television was a young Canadian who had been compelled by rampant anti-Semitism in the comedy world to change his name from Lorne Lipowitz to Lorne Michaels and then eventually to Tom Davis.

In 1975, Tom—or Lorne, as he was still known back then—and I created the groundbreaking late night comedy show *Saturday Night Live*. But mostly it was Lorne/Tom.*

Immediately, *Saturday Night Live* became a sensation. Celebrities, politicians, and intellectuals all wanted to be part of the electric atmosphere at legendary studio 8H in 30 Rockefeller Center. I still remember the night that French intellectual Simone de Beauvoir and I brainstormed "the baseball been berry-berry good to me" routine for Garrett Morris while Buckminster Fuller kibitzed on the sidelines. It was all pretty heady stuff for a shopkeeper's son from Minnesota. The only thing I could compare it to was when our novelty company had been briefly successful.

Though we immediately became media darlings and basked in the adulation of critics and the public alike, don't think for a moment that it was all limousines, oral sex from eager starlets, or oral sex from eager star-

---

*In an effort to keep the book moving along briskly and out of respect for my readers' patience, I have taken the liberty of creating what I call "composite" characters. These composite characters are indicated by two names separated by a slash. For example, "Lorne/Tom" is a composite of several real people, among them Lorne Michaels and Tom Davis.

lets in the back of limousines. It was hard work. On show weeks Lorne/Tom and I routinely put in twenty-hour days, fueled by nothing more than black coffee, stale candy bars, and our own youthful exuberance. By the second week, though, this was beginning to take its toll and we were forced to reuse some of the same characters again and again. It's ironic that one of *Saturday Night Live's* best-loved features, using running characters like the Killer Bees, the Samurai, and the Church Lady in repetitive settings, came about not as the result of a brilliant creative decision but rather as a consequence of sheer exhaustion and crankiness.

Lorne, in his "Tom" persona, and I would also occasionally appear on the show as "Franken and Davis." It was during these moments in front of the camera that I acquired a treasured insight: People really like me. I'm not sure whether it's my winning smile, my light and easy manner, or an indefinable grain of what we in show business call "kismet." But for some reason, audiences respond to anything I do, whether it's commenting on the "Al Franken Decade," reporting live with a satellite dish on my head, or playing my most popular character, the Guy with the Unusually Long Nose Hairs.

THE GUY WITH THE UNUSUALLY LONG NOSE HAIRS—1977.

I soon found that I could no longer walk down the street without being accosted by adoring fans asking me things like: "How's the Al Franken Decade?" or "Where's your satellite dish?" or "What happened to your unusually long nose hairs?"

But there was a dark side to tremendous success at an early age. No, it wasn't the sneaking suspicion that I was a fraud, a talentless hack who happened to be in the right place at the right time. No, it was the long hours, the temptation posed by sexually available groupies, and the guilt I suffered over constantly giving in to the temptation of the sexually available groupies. After a while, these began to take a toll on my marriage.

Did I mention I was married? Right after college I met Franni Bryson. We fell in love, blah, blah, blah.

Although a child of the sixties, Franni harbored some traditional views on the sanctity of marriage, views that I now share in principle. I admit that during the SNL years I caused pain in my marriage. Specifically, the sort of pain that might have been caused if I had been repeatedly unfaithful to my wife and spent a number of holidays and anniversaries away from home in the company of a series of mistresses.

When I decided to run for president, I knew there would come a time when I would have to address this issue. It's become an unfortunate fact of life that anyone running for president in this day and age must not only present a compelling vision for the future of the country, which is time-consuming enough, but also expose his private life to the closest possible scrutiny.

As others have pointed out, I am not perfect. No one is perfect.

Not my opponent, whoever that may be. He or she is just a man, like me. I don't think the American public wants a president who has never had any problems. They want a president who can solve problems. And my wife and I have solved our problems time and time again.

With that in mind I want to set a few ground rules for the forthcoming campaign. First of all, having already acknowledged "causing pain" in my marriage, I will not dignify with an answer any further questions concerning my past, present, or future sexual behavior. This ground rule should not be regarded as an admission that I am currently involved in any improper relationships. It is simply my attempt to elevate the level of discourse beyond the tawdry obsessions of tabloid journalism.

The second ground rule is much like the first ground rule. It is simply that I will not confirm or deny any reports of my involvement in any improper sexual relationships. Again, nothing about this ground rule should be construed as an admission of anything.

Third, I will not be drawn into a debate about what is or what is not a proper sexual relationship or, like I said, whether or not I'm having one. I'm just not going to talk about that.

Fourth, my facial expression while I am listening to other people discuss improper sexual relationships should not be construed one way or the other. Also, I would caution the media against employing body-language experts or voice stress tests in order to determine whether or not I'm having improper sexual relations. If you do, I will sue you.

The next ground rule is a little complicated so please read it carefully. If, at any point during my candidacy or my term in office, I am accused by a woman of having had improper sexual relations with her, my silence should be interpreted as a sincere belief that the woman in question is crazy or a skank or both, although it would not be appropriate for me to say so out loud.

Finally, listing these ground rules in no way precludes my coming up with more ground rules later. For example, here's one: Former members of my staff who claim to have witnessed me in inappropriate situations with female members of my staff should be assumed to be disgruntled former employees with an ax to grind.

Here's another one: If a woman says that I have distinguishing characteristics on my genitals, please don't speculate or make jokes about what those distinguishing characteristics might be. For example, jokes in the form of "the distinguishing characteristic on Al Franken's genitals is a birthmark in the shape of (blank)" would be a violation of this ground rule.

Now that the ground rules are clear, let's get back to my fifteen years of work at *Saturday Night Live*. Some critics might suggest that a career as a writer-producer-performer on a television comedy show is not the kind of background that we need in the Oval Office. Such people are fond of suggesting that a governor or a senator would make a better president than a writer or producer-performer. That simply isn't so. Oh, another ground rule: Don't follow me. I know Gary Hart invited the press to follow him in 1988. But I've spoken with Gary recently, and he now believes that was a mistake. So remember, I've explicitly asked you not to follow me.

My early years at *Saturday Night Live* were the crucible in which was forged a lifelong commitment to excellence. Lorne/Tom had only one rule at *Saturday Night Live:* Whatever it was, it had to be the best, be it a set design, a musical arrangement, the upholstery on a new suite of furniture for his office, the white wine in his personal refrigerator, his summer home in Amagansett, or the prosthetic nose hairs for my beloved character the Guy with the Unusually Long Nose Hairs.

Lorne/Tom also believed strongly in loyalty. And that sometimes caused problems on the excellence front. By Year Eight, the country had grown tired of the Guy with the Unusually Long Nose Hairs. But out of loyalty, misplaced perhaps, Lorne/Tom continued to allow me to perform the character over and over again until Year Twelve, when he produced the movie version.

But some members of the *Saturday Night Live* staff did not share Lorne/Tom's belief in excellence and loyalty. They were only interested in drugs. By Week Three, cocaine had spread like wildfire through the offices on the seventeenth floor. It had two immediate effects on the staff of the show: It gave them a false sense of well-being and it made them want more cocaine. Wanting more cocaine would make the staff irritable until it got more cocaine. Eventually, always desperately wanting more cocaine threatened to become a full-blown addiction.

For my part, I stayed on the sidelines, snorting only the occasional line, so that I could stay awake to make sure the others wouldn't do too much cocaine. Despite my vigilance, one of our number, John Belushi, succumbed to an overdose of drugs after injecting himself with a powerful narcotic, "speedball." The death of my dear friend and colleague helped form my fervent opposition to the legalization of speedballs and all other drugs.

Let's face it, Americans love drugs. Whether it's the card-playing granny who is popping painkillers between hands at the bridge club, or the hard-core junkie scoring a fix on a ghetto street corner, most Americans have drug problems and mine were no worse than most people's. In fact, I believe that a president who has smoked the occasional joint or snorted the occasional line or dropped the occasional tab of acid is better suited for the nation's highest office than someone who has only smoked the occasional joint and not done the other stuff.

I don't want to give the impression that, after a while, all we did on *Saturday Night Live* was drugs. That simply is not the case. These were years of enormous creative fulfillment, an enormously productive time when the show reached the zenith of its power and influence. Some said that the show had become too powerful, that it was wrong for so much power to be concentrated in a single television program. And after the show became less powerful, measures were taken to ensure that no show would ever be that powerful again. Except *Seinfeld*.

When Lorne/Tom abruptly up and left the program in the summer of 1984, many of us felt cut adrift. Lorne/Tom had become a sort of surrogate father to me, replacing the man who had been taken years before by a dentist's poorly regulated gas canister. Without Lorne/Tom at my side, I learned firsthand what it means to be lonely—with only your wife and children for companionship. But I also learned a valuable lesson about independence, about standing on one's own two feet and about saying good-bye once and for all to the emotional crutch of hiding behind a character, like the Guy with the Unusually Long Nose Hairs.

It was a long time before I would find another character as compelling and "edgy" as the nose hair guy. And, when I finally did find that character, it was really more that he found me rather than the other way around of me finding him.

I'm often asked if Stuart Smalley is based on a real person. He is. I first encountered Stewart Smiley at an Al-Anon meeting, which I had gone to in hopes of encountering an interesting character to use in my act. For a comedian, the great thing about twelve-step programs is that they are an endless source of amusing anecdotes from real people. But I also believe in twelve-step programs and the principles on which they are based, including anonymity, which is why I changed the name of the real Stewart Smiley, who frankly has a lot of serious problems, to Stuart Smalley, and made him less effeminate.

STUART SMALLEY   STEWART SMILEY

Stuart Smalley took the country by storm, allowing me to put the Guy With the Unusually Long Nose Hairs behind me once and for all. After perfecting the character by adding a wig to make me look more like the real Stewart Smiley, I went on the road playing colleges, nightclubs, and, eventually, amphitheaters. A book offer followed, requiring me to return to New York, where I could surreptitiously tape-record the real Stewart Smiley as he "shared" his ever-worsening problems with us at Al-Anon. I wasn't able to use any material about how crazy it was making him to have me doing an impression of him, which is too bad because he talked about it a lot.

When the book came out, Stewart stopped coming to Al-Anon alto-gether, which prevented me from writing a sequel, and I began to notice that others in my Al-Anon meeting were less willing to share amusing anecdotes when I was around. But as luck would have it, the character had caught the eye of film producer Don Simpson, and I spent the next year working on an action movie where Stuart saves his family after they are kidnapped and held hostage by a gang of narco-terrorists. I still think that version would have worked if only Simpson hadn't been so fucked up and had been able to concentrate on it a little more.

When Simpson died, the project was picked up by Paramount and rewritten as a sensitive "dramedy," and became one of the films of 1995. It was my first foray into the movie business. I liked it. More important, the world liked it. Films like *Terminator 2, Lethal Weapon,* and *Stuart Saves His Family* contribute over 4 billion dollars annually to America's balance of trade, second only to agriculture and aerospace.

As a player in the global economy of the 1990s, I've come to accept the interconnectedness of all peoples and cultures on Earth—while realiz-ing that some films don't necessarily "play" in every market. As president, I would strengthen America's position as the leader in world trade by ex-panding our involvement in regional trading blocs such as NAFTA and by using my fast-track negotiating authority to push for a lowering of anti-competitive trade restrictions worldwide. If that didn't work, I would raise tariffs to punish countries that refuse to open their markets to American products. Now, if that still didn't do the trick, I would heavily subsidize domestic industries so that they could undersell just about anybody, dri-ving weaker nations' industries out of business.

The point is I am for free trade, and I am for fair trade, unless, of course, America is getting the better of the deal, and then I'm mostly for free trade.

Whenever I tell people that I'm running for president, they act sur-prised. Why, they want to know, would I squander the respect I've earned in my climb to the pinnacle of show business? The answer is very simple. It's time to give something back.

CHAPTER SIX

MY FIRST EXPERIENCE IN GIVING SOMETHING BACK

My first experience in giving something back worked out very well. In the wake of the Contract with America and the Republican takeover of Congress in 1994, I decided to write a bestseller that would alert America to the dangers of Newt Gingrich and his gang of thugs.

The first thing any writer has to do when preparing to write a bestseller is to find the best possible team for the job at hand. I interviewed Judith Krantz's team, John Grisham's team, and Team Tom Clancy, none of whom were right for the job. This meant one thing. I would have to assemble my own team from scratch to begin work on the book, then tentatively titled *Rush Limbaugh's Butt Is Big and Smelly.*

For policy, I went to Norm Ornstein of the American Enterprise Institute, the top policy guy in the business. For research, there was Geoff Rodkey and a group of young Harvard graduates, affectionately known as the "Nexis Gang." For writing I brought in Nobel prize–winner Saul Bellow. But his approach didn't work. Neither did Isaac Bashevis Singer's. These were dark days. But after a few false starts I settled upon a method that seemed to work and that, I think, will become the standard for all books written in the future.

We would begin with a policy document drafted by Norm. Geoff and his crew would add facts and figures. Then, our writers' room, consisting of Kurt Vonnegut, Tom Pynchon, and Singer, who was, frankly, deadwood, but he was old and needed the money, would pound out a rough draft. Then, I would look it over.

Vonnegut and Pynchon did commendable work, and even old Singer would get a line or two in now and then. But they weren't funny, at least not ha-ha laugh-out-loud funny like the Guy with the Unusually Long Nose Hairs had been. There was only one solution: I would have to write the book myself.

But that didn't work either. My publisher, Delacorte, felt that my version, while entertaining, was much too short, and that people would not be willing to pay $21.95 for a book that was only thirty-seven pages long.

It was time for radical surgery. Vonnegut, Pynchon, and the rest were out. In came a team of comedy all-stars, headed up by legendary twelve-time Emmy-winning humor guru Jim Downey. Jim wouldn't write as such but he would inspire and organize the group, which included *Simpsons* scribe George Meyer, whose unique sense of the absurd found fertile ground in the world of politics. Author and James Bond screenwriter Bruce Fierstein, though expensive, proved he was worth every penny when he suggested poking fun at Al D'Amato as well as Rush Limbaugh and Newt Gingrich. Adding seasoning to the delectable stew served up by Jim and his comedy cooks was a handful of comedy veterans headed by my old friend Earl Pomerantz. Work proceeded apace, though not quick enough for Delacorte, and it soon became necessary to put on a night shift of writers under Robert Smigel, whose animated extravaganzas have enlivened recent seasons of *Saturday Night Live*.

All in all they were a good group, the best that money could buy, and with their hard work a solid foundation for the book was beginning to emerge. I often reflected, as I watched my writers through the glass door separating my office from theirs, that I owed them a great deal. I am not exaggerating when I say that the book simply could not have been written without them.

There was a missing piece of the puzzle, though—a final element that proved to be the keystone of the entire enterprise: the title. My writers had come up with many, including *Rush Limbaugh Won't Like This Book, Newt Gingrich's Butt Is Bigger and Smellier Than Rush Limbaugh's,* and *The Guy with the Incredibly Long Nose Hairs' Guide to Life.*

After a week of round-the-clock brainstorming, I angrily dismissed my writers and went into seclusion at the Crillon Hotel in Paris. Fueled by coffee and foie gras, I drove the hotel staff mad with my requests for paper and pencils at all hours of the day and night. Finally, I had it. But then returning home on the Concorde, I forgot it, only to check my pockets and find a piece of paper with "Rush Limbaugh Is a Big Fat Idiot" on it. That wasn't it. But it would have to do.

Rush Limbaugh Is a Big Fat Idiot became a number-one bestseller for more than a hundred weeks. More than that, it stopped the Gingrich-Limbaugh-Robertson-Pataki gang dead in their tracks. The Republican Revolution was over, and it was I, Al Franken, who had driven the stake through its hard, black, and tiny heart.*

My writers and I had stemmed the deadly right-wing tide in the nick of time, saving such essential programs as Medicare, Social Security, and the National Endowment for the Arts. Next time you and your family are enjoying an exhibit of Robert Mapplethorpe photos of gay men defecating on each other, remember that if it were not for my book, you would have had to pay a hefty admission fee.

As the bestselling author of a book that had changed the course of American history, I was roundly feted in intellectual, artistic, and political circles. It's the sort of thing that would have gone to a lesser man's head, but my ever-growing entourage was there to keep me grounded.

It wasn't long before an invitation came from the White House to consult President Clinton on matters ranging from domestic policy to foreign affairs to jokes about his eating a lot of Big Macs. There, up close in the room, I got to take the measure of the man who has been called the smartest Democratic politician ever, indeed, the smartest *person* ever, period. I think that's overstating it, but he is very smart.

------

*Several years later, I encountered Limbaugh at a party. He was drunk, of course, but nonetheless very pleasant and seemed to bear no hard feelings about my book, which had included a number of personal ad hominem insults regarding his size, along with the attacks on his so-called philosophy. He put a hammy arm around my shoulders and said, "Franken, you are one funny little Jew-boy. Hey, pull my finger!"

"Uh, no thanks, Rush. I don't think I really want to pull your finger."

"Fine then, I'll pull it myself." True to his word, Rush pulled his own finger, releasing an enormous cloud of intensely foul gas out of the seat of his XXXL khakis. Although his behavior was almost unimaginably crude, I have to give the man credit: he was simply too big to hold a grudge and even offered me sloppy seconds with one of his hookers.

Still, I found myself diving in with suggestions for improvements on many of his more far-fetched schemes, like providing tax credits for child care. There, amidst policy wonks and spin doctors like George Stephanopoulos, Rahm Emanuel, Hillary Clinton, and Leon Panetta, I felt in my element; and though it would be bragging to say that I was better than all of the President's other advisors put together, I was certainly better than any of them individually.

As a key member of the policy team that crafted the agenda that led to seven years of unprecedented economic growth, as well as a very funny speech to the Gridiron Club, I found I was devoting more and more of my time to politics. I was forced to leave the writing of my book's sequel to my writing staff, which soon fell apart without my leadership. This was not the first sacrifice I would make for Bill Clinton, who, though smart, as I've said, is not exactly the most grateful guy around.

Being a White House insider had its shocking and unseemly side. This was brought home to me every time I would encounter Al Gore, whose uncontrollable libido and inappropriate sexual behavior toward anything with two legs and a hole in between brought shame and ill-repute to Bill Clinton's presidency.

Gore's one-track mind afforded little room for contemplation of issues not related to his dick. I remember Gore leaving a meeting to go chase girls after a particularly unimpressive performance. I turned to Panetta, rolled my eyes, and asked, "Is it just me? Or is that guy a complete zero?" Panetta confirmed my worst suspicions about the vice president, saying something to the effect that putting him on the ticket had been a big mistake.

This is the man who had supposedly "reinvented" government. And yet when I looked around Washington, I saw the same government I had always seen: the White House, the Capitol, the National Air and Space Museum. Where was all this reinventing that the vice president had touted so highly? Nowhere I could see. Panetta didn't seem to know where it was either.

And yet Al Gore is supposed to carry our party's standard into the new millennium. That is, if he can take the time away from his endless womanizing to fill out the necessary documents.

Also, Tipper's no prize. But indulging in personal attacks is not the "Franken style." I wish I could say that personal attacks are also not a part of the "Gore style," but like many Americans, I believe Gore to be willing to do anything, no matter how dishonest or illegal, to get elected. So, Al, if you're reading this, I pledge to you and the American people, that I will match you blow for blow if you try and pull this campaign down into the gutter.

If you, for instance, call me "unqualified," I will respond by calling you "unqualified." If you call me a "bastard" or a "cocksucker," I will call you the very same thing. If you attack my family, particularly my children by, say, calling them "dumb" or "spoiled," I think you know what I'll do. Yes. I will criticize your children and call them names, also.

There. Now that we're clear, the campaign can proceed. May the best man win.

CHAPTER SEVEN

DARING TO DREAM

In February 1998, I returned home to Christhaven and walked the streets of its revitalized downtown. I stopped outside what had once been Franken's Department Store and was now a Radio Shack.

Exchanging smiles and suspicious glances with passersby, I looked for a sign from the spirit of my late father, which I felt certain must haunt these precincts, as to whether or not I should take the momentous step I was currently contemplating.

There, in the window of Radio Shack, was the sign I was looking for. It was a sign announcing a "President's Day Sale-a-bration." The visages of Washington and Lincoln stared down at me, and perhaps it was a trick of the light but they seemed to be smiling. "Run, Al, run!" Lincoln seemed to say. "Yes, Al, do as Lincoln says, and run for president!" Washington appeared to concur. That was all I needed to seem to hear.

Above Lincoln and Washington a third face, that of Roger DeSalles, chairman of the Tandy Corporation, Radio Shack's parent company, was smiling too, indicating that my campaign would enjoy the support of the influential business community. I made up my mind then and there, standing in front of what had been my father's pride and joy and the source of his ultimate ruin, to run for president.

The decision in many ways was the easiest decision I ever made in my life. What I didn't know then was how much hard work would lie ahead, and just how draining a campaign for the presidency would be. But since that decisive moment in Christhaven, through the good times and the hard times, I have sustained myself in the certain knowledge that Al Franken should be president. Why not me? Why not me?

Why not me?

PART TWO

THE CAMPAIGN

(Embargoed until 12:00 p.m. Eastern
Standard Time, March 24, 1999.)

Statement of Al Franken, Candidate for President of the United States

Ladies and gentlemen, members of the media,
friends and neighbors from Christhaven, and spe-
cially bussed-in seniors . . .

I stand before you today, a humble native son,
to ask your support as I embark upon what I am
told will be a long journey. The calendar tells
us that there are 594 or so days between today
and the presidential election next November. But
there are more than just days separating us from
our destination. There are miles, there are people,
and there are dangerous preconceptions about who
can and can't be president. Of the United States.

Now, as for the miles, I've got that covered.
You know what they say about us Minnesotans. All
we need is a pair of snowshoes, some dry underwear, and a good reason, and we'll be there
before nightfall. Well, I've still got my snowshoes (MR. FRANKEN HOLDS UP BATTERED SNOWSHOES),
my underwear is reasonably dry, and I've got the
best possible reason in the world: you. You are
my reason. (PAUSE FOR APPLAUSE)

But you are not the only people I need in my
corner. You are few.

And we need many. But if each of you leave here
today and you tell two friends, and they tell two
friends, and they tell two friends, and so on and
so on, soon we will have the majority we need to
impose our will upon the entrenched interests and
to let them know that politics as usual will only
get you politicians as usual. (PAUSE FOR APPLAUSE)

As for the dangerous preconceptions about what

sort of a man—or woman—(PAUSE FOR APPLAUSE) is fit for our highest office, let me say that the pundits, the pollsters, and the party pooh-bahs have already made up your minds for you. But I believe that you are smarter than they think you are. They think you're a bunch of stupid drooling morons. I beg to differ. (PAUSE FOR APPLAUSE)

The pundits, for starters, are complete frauds. To the pundits I have only one thing to say: Who elected you? No one. No one elected you. No one! No one!! NO ONE!!! (ANTICIPATE CROWD CHANTING ALONG)

As for the pollsters, their precious polls say that I can't win. But that's not what the people say. They say the polls are wrong. They say that I can win and that I will win! (PAUSE FOR APPLAUSE) And I say to the pollsters that until you start polling some real Americans, your margin of error will be 100 percent! (PAUSE FOR APPLAUSE)

As for the party bosses who have already written me off, you're in for a very unpleasant surprise. When I win this party's nomination, you'll see who's boss. That's right. It's not you. It's the people and their leader, me. (PAUSE FOR APPLAUSE)

In the days, weeks, and months ahead, you will be hearing more from me about my specific plan for your future. But first, I want to hear what you have to say. And that's why immediately after this speech, I will be leaving for New Hampshire, where I intend to walk the state diagonally, and then from side to side, visiting every single household.

But when I do put my plan before you, I think that you will see that I know something about what issues are important to ordinary Americans. It'll be a plan full of ideas—like lower ATM fees—that resonate in the heartland. Why should hardworking Americans shell out a dollar each time they want

to make a deposit into their savings account?
Banks don't need the money. People do.
(PAUSE FOR APPLAUSE)

Lower ATM fees is just one of the visionary ele-
ments of my specific plan. One of many. But it is
still early in the campaign, and I want to run
some things by the voters in New Hampshire before
I formally commit to them. (PAUSE FOR APPLAUSE)

Finally, I pledge to you today, here, a stone's
throw from the hospital in which I was born, that
if I am elected there will be no major scandals
during my administration. I'm not saying there will
be no scandals whatsoever. No candidate can honestly make that pledge. Any honest candidate, and
I consider myself one of those, must admit that
there will be a certain level of ongoing scandal.
There's no getting around that. The important thing
is to recognize the scandals as they come up, accept them, and try to manage each scandal individually so that it does not get out of hand. That's
the kind of straightforwardness and attention to
detail you can expect from a Franken Administration, and you should accept nothing less from any
other candidate. (PAUSE FOR APPLAUSE)

And so, my friends, we begin a long journey,
trusting in God and our fellow man, though more
in God. If I would ask one thing of you here today, it would not be that you donate money, though
that would be nice, or that you tell your friends
about me, although as I said earlier that would
help a lot too, it would be that you pray for God
to show me the way that I might win. Thank you.
We'll see you on election night in 452 days or so.

The New York Times

Corrections

—Due to an editing error, the name of Democratic presidential hopeful Al Frankerl was misspelled as "Al Franklin" in yesterday's *New York Times*. Mr. Frankerl is not, as the article said, "the former governor general of Bermuda." That is Alistair, Earl of Frank. The article also quoted an unnamed bystander who described Mr. Frankerl's platform as "a bizarre admixture of vacuous catchphrases and vague, formless attacks on some imagined status quo by an obscure political parvenu." The reporter should have identified the bystander as *Times* columnist William Safire, who happened to be in Minnesota to visit his former college roommate who was recently diagnosed with non-Hodgkin's lymphoma, which is almost invariably fatal in its late stages. The *Times* regrets the errors and apologizes unconditionally to Mr. Frankerl.

■

—Due to a reporting error, an article in yesterday's *Times* about the watchdog group Accuracy for Media misquoted University of Pennsylvania professor Kathleen Hall Jamieson as saying, "Newspapers always make their mistakes on page thirty-eight and print their corrections on page one." What Professor Jamieson actually said was, "Newspapers always make their mistakes on page one and print their corrections on page thirty-eight." For the complete corrected text of the article, please turn to page 38.

■

FROM *THIS WEEK WITH SAM DONALDSON AND COKIE ROBERTS*, MARCH 28, 1999

SAM DONALDSON: Also rounding out the field of nuts, flakes, and fruits who always seem to come out of the woodwork in this, the silly season before the real campaign for president can begin, is comedian and author Al Franken. (LAUGHTER)

GEORGE WILL: You know, William Pitt the Elder said that the people get the leaders they deserve. Maybe if Americans were willing to put up with eight years of Bill Clinton, they deserve someone as wholly unqualified as Al Franken. (LAUGHTER)

COKIE ROBERTS: Well, let's talk about Al Franken for a second. He said one thing that really made sense to me.

SAM: Oh, come on, Cokie! You know very well that he didn't say a single thing that made a lick of sense!

COKIE: Well, I admit most of it was just random blather, but at one point he said something about ATM fees being too high. And I agree with that.

GEORGE: Oh, piffle. When the voters go to the polls to exercise the democratic prerogatives that our forefathers fought and died for, I hope they have more on their minds than ATM fees.

SAM: I don't know, George. Maybe Cokie's got a point here. I mean, everyone uses an ATM from time to time. Even you. Right, George?

GEORGE: No, actually, Sam, I use a small private bank that just brings me a stack of new bills whenever I need them.

COKIE: Well, I use one all the time. And I resent paying a dollar each time I need some cash to go to the beauty parlor.

SAM: Well, you look beautiful. So it was worth it. (LAUGHTER) Let's bring George Stephanopoulos and

BILL KRISTOL: Sam, the fact that Franken is able to run on the single issue of ATM fees proves conclusively that the Democratic party is completely and utterly intellectually bankrupt.

GEORGE STEPHANOPOULOS: Bill, you know very well the Republicans would never support lower ATM fees because the big banking interests that pay you guys millions of dollars a year in soft money would never allow it. You know you're vulnerable on this, and you just wish you had an issue as good as ATM fees.

BILL: George, are you saying that I'm afraid of Al Franken?

STEPHANOPOULOS: Bill, what I'm saying is that you are afraid of what Al Franken represents.

SAM: Well, I think we're all afraid of that. But let's just be clear, the fee only applies when you use a so-called foreign ATM, an ATM from a bank which is not your own.

STEPHANOPOULOS: That's right, Sam. And that's something Franken will have to deal with if his campaign ever gathers any momentum. You know, I met Al Franken a few years ago when he visited the White House to help Bill Clinton with a few jokes for the annual Gridiron Dinner, and he's a pretty personable guy, very sure of himself.

SAM: Well, I'm not so sure Rush Limbaugh would agree with you, George. (LAUGHTER)

COKIE: Well, we have to take a break here for a word from our old friend David Brinkley.

CUT TO:

DAVID BRINKLEY SITTING IN AN ARMCHAIR
IN A LABORATORY

BRINKLEY: For years I've had the unique privilege
of being invited into your homes each week to
talk to you about the important issues of the day.
Starting this week, as spokesperson for Depends,
I'm going to be talking to you about another important issue: incontinence. What causes incontinence? I don't know. If I did know, I'd tell you.
But I don't. What's more, I don't know who knows.
If I did, I'd ask. I know the Depends people won't
tell me what causes incontinence, because if they
did, I probably wouldn't have to use their product. I first heard of Depends from an old friend,
Dwayne Andreas, chairman of Archer Daniels Midland.
He's not incontinent. He's just too busy to get
up and go to the bathroom. Why? I don't know.
But maybe it's because Archer Daniels Midland
is working day and night to feed a hungry world.
But I'm not here to talk about Archer Daniels
Midland. I'm here to talk about Depends. Depends:
if you're busy like my old friend Dwayne Andreas
or just lazy like Bruce Willis. Back to you,
Sam and Cokie.

CAMPAIGN DIARY

THE FOLLOWING EXCERPTS WERE RELEASED IN MAY 2001, AFTER THE SUPREME COURT RULED UNANIMOUSLY THAT PRESIDENT FRANKEN'S DIARIES WERE NOT PROTECTED BY EXECUTIVE PRIVILEGE

March 31, 1999

Weather continues to be terrible. Want to get hands on asshole who came up with "walking the state" idea. Mud. Also snow. Also people in New Hampshire incredibly stupid. Visited grotesque old lady and man who wanted to talk about Medicare but had lost dentures. Yuck! Think woman will vote for me; man on fence.

April 2, 1999

Think may have to kick Otto off the campaign even though he's brother. Gave me more bad advice when drunk yesterday. Said I should go moose hunting with local newspaper editor. Scared shitless to be in woods with goober carrying high-powered rifle. When moose charged, I hoped it would kill him but came after me and I had to run.

April 3, 1999

Showed Otto picture in newspaper of me running from moose. He was drunk and didn't understand embarrassment potential. Said I look "athletic" and that animal rights people will like the fact that I dropped my gun, ran, and climbed tree instead of shooting moose. I said that Otto was fired but he just laughed as did others in bar. Perhaps should have campaign manager who is not drunk all the time. Called Norm Ornstein.

April 5, 1999

Norm arrived today. Thinks moose incident will be good for the campaign. Advised me to make self-deprecating moose jokes at Elks Club in New Bundleton. Routine about first photo ever of "moose chasing chicken" got big laugh. Elks seemed to think slogan of "Vote for the Chicken" funny also, and said they will vote for me. Norm happy to keep Otto around as "idea man."

April 6, 1999

Am being stalked by insane "Franken for President" guys in foam rubber moose hats. Don't understand why they let New Hampshire pick the president when entire state is full of inbred retards. "Chicken" thing picking up steam.

April 7, 1999

Joel Kleinbaum, lawyer who handled the paperwork on my S-Corp, arrived today to serve as chief counsel for flat rate rather than hourly fee. First thing he said is not to keep diary since it can be subpoenaed later. But fact that he told me so is privileged. Told him he was being paranoid. Otto agrees.

April 9, 1999

Otto and Joel not getting along. Otto threw heavy beer mug at Joel when Joel asked him to sign nondisclosure agreement. Joel afraid Otto will trade campaign secrets for alcohol. I resolved to keep Otto pretty much out of the loop, which will solve that problem.

April 10, 1999

Norm has come up with very impressive campaign strategy document in three-hole-punch binder. Asked him to explain it to me during long walk from Little Northton to Center Conway in driving sleet storm. Didn't see a soul except emergency road crews all day. I hardly notice bad weather now but it was very hard on Norm. Norm particularly did not like having to take shit next to road and wipe ass with wet leaves. Said it was not "presidential," whatever that means.

FRANKEN FOR PRESIDENT

MEMO: HOW YOU CAN WIN

TO: AL FRANKEN

FROM: NORM ORNSTEIN

First, it is important to remember that there is a very good chance you will not win. The current frontrunner, Vice President Gore, enjoys a generous margin over all contenders including yourself. Gore has several advantages: name recognition, the constant visibility of incumbency, his perceived success as part of a "winning team" for the last eight years, as well as the all-important capacity to raise almost unlimited funds.

You do not enjoy any of these advantages.

Gore has one major disadvantage: He is the heavy favorite. This makes him vulnerable in the "expectations" game. If, for example, in a head-to-head race between you and Al Gore in Iowa, Gore gets less than 90 percent of the vote, that will be a victory for you.

At that point, you will become a possible "spoiler" and begin to receive media attention whether or not you really deserve it. By then, the press is sure to be desperate for any fresh angle on what promises to be one of the dullest races for the Democratic nomination in recent memory. You may well become a media darling and can use your moment in the spotlight to set forth the Franken agenda before a national audience.

By that time, then, we must have an agenda.

That is why we should continue to build on the foundation of the ATM fee issue. I have identified a small number of similar issues that will have strong middle-class appeal, such as cable TV rates, car insurance premiums, and car reregistration fees. Any of these issues could prove as incendiary as ATM fees, but since their number is limited you must be cautious to pace yourself and dole these out at widely spaced intervals.

The "spoiler" scenario assumes that you will be taking on Gore one-on-one. However, there are other potential candidates, many of whom share some or all of the advantages that Gore has over a candidate such as yourself. They include House Minority Leader Dick Gephardt, (very strong), former New Jersey senator and basketball star Bill Bradley (very strong), Nebraska senator and war hero Bob Kerrey (strong also), and liberal Minnesota senator Paul Wellstone (weak).

Our best hope is that these other candidates are intimidated by Gore's overwhelming strength and stay out of the race, thus opening the field for a dark horse such as yourself.

In a multicandidate race it is even more crucial to differentiate yourself by reiterating your position on ATM fees over and over again, and to avoid being drawn into debates on complex policy matters in which you would certainly be bested.

A good offensive strategy assumes that all your potential opponents (except Wellstone) have taken money from large corporate interests and super-wealthy individuals, none of whom can be expected to donate anything to you.

These big donors don't do this out of the goodness of their hearts. They do it because they expect something in return. Hopefully, these corporate interests will include banks, which as you are so fond of pointing out collect the fees charged at ATMs. If your campaign were to be summarized in a political cartoon, picture Don Quixote (you) charging at a windmill (the banks). Although Don Quixote was crazy (and not crazy like a fox, just crazy), he is every bit as beloved as the banks are detested.

I guess what I'm saying is stay focused for now on the ATM issue, which will put you in a strategically advantageous position if Gore happens to self-destruct.

In summary, our initial strategy should have three parts: define the message (ATM fees), refine the message (ATM fees), and repeat the message (ATM fees). If you follow this simple strategy, you'll be able to keep your head above-water, while awaiting a miracle.

Best,

Norm

April 11, 1999

Norm severely frostbitten after night at unimproved national park campsite. Think he may lose toe. Norm says if more than one toe is amputated he will quit campaign. That would be a disaster since I would have to spend all my time with Otto, who is always drunk, and Joel, who is big worrywart and keeps bugging me not to keep diary. I promised him I will use special "code" from now on.

April 12, 1999

Asked N about J's worries about diary. N thinks code is good idea.

April 13, 1999

Great news! O says ATM issue catching fire with people he talks to in New Hampshire bars. Also, doctors saved N's toe.

April 14, 1999

N thinks we should hold "teach-in" at Boynton's Corners Community Center on ATMs and ATM fees. I agreed, provided it was very simplistic and dumbed-down for local stupid people ("S.P."). J still on my back about diary. I told him to spend more time bailing O out of jail and less time being a mother hen.

April 15, 1999

J bitching and moaning about my forgetting to file taxes today. J says that presidential candidates should file tax returns on time. Checked with N. N says this is true. Called my wife ("F") and yelled at her for forty-five minutes about tax return. Felt good.

April 16, 1999

ATM teach-in big success despite audience of wall-to-wall S.P. Think they call this the Granite State because that is what the heads of the people who live here are made of. Ha ha. Here's a for instance: During Q&A one idiot asked me if banks made profit on fees or whether they merely offset the costs of installing and maintaining the machines. I told her that that was not the point.

That shut the old cow up. Asked N later how long campaign will continue. He said Primary is not until February of next year! Don't think I can handle another ten months of New Hampshire and its S.P.

April 17, 1999

Still on a high from last night's teach-in, knocked off record number of houses today (eleven). Discussed possibility of backing out on misguided plan to walk state with N. He suggests not going back to houses where no one is home because that slows us down considerably. Great idea, N!

April 18, 1999

With new "no going back" rule, hit sixteen houses. Would have been twenty if moronic dairy farmer hadn't tricked me into "milking" bull. After twenty minutes of "milking" with little result, decided I didn't need farmer's vote that bad.

April 19, 1999

N furious about picture of me "milking" bull in *Cloverdale Junction Bugle.* Says if Associated Press picks it up, no amount of self-destructing on Gore's part could help us. O and friends bought all copies of paper and threw them down wishing well at abandoned amusement park. To avoid repeat, N insists I remain with him at all times, even when he goes to bathroom, which will be time-consuming since he has been constipated since incident on side of road with wet leaves.

April 20, 1999

Only seven houses today. Slowed down by 2 hr. 45 min. stop in Mobil station men's room with Norm. Did speak in men's room to three people whose houses we no longer have to visit. May be more efficient to let voters come to us, though having Norm on toilet may not be putting best foot forward.

April 21, 1999

My turn to be mad at Norm for humiliating photo of me in gas station bathroom. Dickhead reporter from *Easting Falls Gazette* said I did not wash hands, which is complete bullshit.

April 22, 1999

Campaign in crisis. Otto tracked down *Easting Falls Gazette* reporter and coldcocked him with two-by-four. Reporter in coma. No witnesses. Joel says we must turn Otto in, but Otto disagrees. Norm in toilet. Time for me to show some leadership.

April 23, 1999

Rented car. Led my team out of Easting Falls to entirely different part of state. Joel stuck on subject on subject of diary like broken record. Must remember to go back to using code. Got J to shut up about diary by agreeing to turn in O to police if reporter dies. O suggests framing J instead. Have to make difficult decision. Keeping N in dark.

April 24, 1999

Wow! Should have rented a car sooner! It makes "walking" much easier. Thirty-five houses today.

April 25, 1999

Great news! Reporter out of coma. Remembers nothing. We're on a roll!

April 26, 1999

N thinks it is time to bring media consultant on board. But O objects to fifth person in car. J suggest upgrading rental to midsize. Typical J! Always ready to spend my money. O wonders what media consultant could do that O hasn't done already. J makes crack about media consultant bringing his own two-by-four. O buys six-pack of tall boys at 7-Eleven and sulks.

April 27, 1999

Big lift for Franken campaign today! Got stuck right in the middle of Gore's motorcade when fuel pump on rent-a-car broke down. Secret Service swarming everywhere while state troopers pushed our car off the road so Gore could get past. Caught glimpse of him when he stuck head out of window to see what the problem was. Everyone excited by taste of the big time, even gloomy Joel.

April 28, 1999

Still on cloud nine from successful encounter with Gore. Also mechanic and tow truck driver both promise to vote for me. Tow truck guy even offered to put "Franken for President" bumper sticker on back of tow truck. If only we had bumper stickers! Joel getting bids from local printers. Great way to keep him off my back about diary. Musn't forget code.

April 29, 1999

Ran into Gore again today. Franken 2, Gore 0. Joked to N that Gore should stop following me around. N laughed, so called F and told her joke. She bugged me about taxes, so I put her on with J. O, meanwhile, had infiltrated Gore rally in South Cutely. O asked four or five questions about ATM fees before being removed. Gore handled first two questions but was clearly rattled by the fourth or fifth. Way to go, O!

April 30, 1999

The Boston Globe

Tough Questions for Gore in New Hampshire

SOUTH CUTELY, N.H., April 29— The campaign of Vice President Al Gore ran into a speed bump here today when Gore was peppered by embarrassing questions regarding his relationship with large banking interests. Gore's handlers were spinning like dervishes by nightfall, trying to portray the event as a welcome give-and-take and "democracy at work."

It remains to be seen, however, whether there may be long-term damage from the vice president's awkward and unconvincing answers to a series of questions posed by a local man who identified himself as Botto Branken and gave his occupation as manure farmer.

Branken demanded to know where the vice president stood on the issue of ATM fees and in particular whether he opposes them categorically like dark horse candidate Al Franken does. Gore seemed at first unfamiliar with both the issue of the unpopular

(continued on next page)

(continued from previous page) fees and with candidate Franken and stumbled with a vague and rambling response.

Unsatisfied, Branken demanded to know whether Gore had ever taken money from banks that charge ATM fees. In an apparent effort to move past the issue of banks and ATM fees altogether, Gore indignantly insisted that "not one dollar spent by consumers at ATMs has ever found its way into my campaign, and if anyone can prove otherwise, I'll eat my hat."

Immediately following the event, Gore's deputy campaign manager Ron Klane issued a clarifying statement that read in part: "Although the Vice President has received donations from banks and banking industry lobbying groups, it is reasonable to say that none of this money came directly from ATM fees."

However, banking industry analyst Peter Steingarten of the American Enterprise Institute called such a claim "preposterous on its face and totally disingenuous" because "even banks are not able to track individual dollars as they move from a consumer's pocket to Al Gore's."

Gore's media consultant, Bob Squier, conceded that Gore may have erred in answering the question the way he did, but that it was "an honest mistake from an honest candidate who's working up an appetite to eat that hat like he promised." Squier was then hit on the head with a board by a passerby.

At press time the Franken campaign could not be located for comment.

May 1, 1999

We may just win this thing! N's friend Peter Steingarten says Gore very vulnerable on bank issue. N says Peter ("P") very needy and insecure and can be bought with flattery and/or cabinet position. But N peeved about missing phone call from *Boston Globe* after J ran down cell phone battery talking to kids. O insists cell phone can run off car battery and pulled wires out of dashboard but only succeeded in making left blinker flash constantly. Finally, decided to take "special offer" from Radio Shed, a local rip-off of Radio Shack, to buy cell phone for 1 cent if I agree to sign up for AT&T wireless service at sixty dollars a month. Some offer! Real "special"!

May 2, 1999

Norm had brainstorm. Send Otto to Iowa to taunt Gore with hat. Made Otto promise not to hit Gore campaign staff or media with board.

May 3, 1999

Otto called from Iowa. Collect. Very excited about disrupting Gore rally. Difficult to get details because Otto drunk and incoherent. Also slurring. Joel very nervous about Otto. Also diary. Will use code from now on.

May 4, 1999

𝕿𝖍𝖊 𝕯𝖊𝖘 𝕸𝖔𝖎𝖓𝖊𝖘 𝕽𝖊𝖌𝖎𝖘𝖙𝖊𝖗

Local Man Throws Gore for Loop with Tough Questions

Muscatine, Iowa, May 3—The Gore campaign hit another snag today when the vice president appeared rattled by a local man who disrupted a rally here with more embarrassing questions about Gore's connection with large banking interests. The man, Dotto Dranken, a local manure farmer, has dogged the Gore campaign throughout its stay in Iowa by appearing at rallies dressed as a giant hat. Dranken repeatedly challenged the vice president to live up to a promise made in New Hampshire to "eat [his] hat" if anyone could prove that any ATM fees had found their way into his campaign war chest.

Wearing a large sign reading "Eat me," Dranken taunted Gore at three separate appearances today by shouting, "Tell the truth, ATM stooge," "Gore's a whore," and "Eat me." The image of the vice president reddened and sputtering furiously was carried on all three network newcasts.

The issue of bank contributions to the Gore campaign threatens to undermine the vice president's hard-won image as a straight arrow since it carries echoes of the campaign finance scandals of 1996. Peter Steingarten of the American Enterprise Institute, an expert on *(continued on next page)*

(continued from previous page)
bank industry lobbying efforts, described the matter as "a skeleton in Gore's closet that could turn out to be the skeleton of a *Tyrannosaurus rex.*" What Steingarten seemed to be saying was that what some are already calling "ATM-gate" could turn into a big problem for Gore, a point Steingarten made using the metaphor of a *Tyrannosaurus rex,* the carnivorous dinosaur that was one of the very largest of the late Cretaceous era.

Gore's communications director, Bob Squier, who is recovering in a New Hampshire hospital from a blow to the head, attempted to downplay the whole issue but was too nauseous to do so effectively. Reached by phone, Squier said, "Al Gore has proved time and again during his twenty-five-year career in public life that he . . . oh . . . he . . . excuse me."

Describing himself as a "Franken Democrat," Dranken pledged to turn up at every Gore event until the vice president makes good on his promise to eat his hat. "Iowa voters like me don't want a crook like Al Gore in the White House. They want a candidate like Al Franken," said Dranken.

The Franken campaign could not be located for comment.

May 4, 1999

Norm livid about missing phone call from *Des Moines Register.* What happened was Franni called to tell me Otto was on CBS and stupid Radio Shed phone does not have call-waiting. This "special offer" is beginning to look less and less "special" all the time. Caught Otto on TV in house of local Stupid People. Joel almost had nervous breakdown. Beginning to wonder if Joel is right for job of campaign counsel. Made me swear not to write about Otto in diary. Okay, "J"!

May 5, 1999

Ain't no stoppin' us now! MSNBC producer reached us on cell phone while we were in car "walking" through White Mountain National Forest. Wanted to schedule appearance about ATM-gate. Just before cell phone connection lost, made plan to appear via satellite from Manchester. Hooray!

TRANSCRIPT OF MSNBC CABLECAST—May 6, 1999

SOLEDAD O'BRIEN: Joining us now is comedian and Democratic presidential candidate Al Franken. Al, welcome. Also with us are our regular panelists: Internet entrepreneur Omar Wasow, Republican strategist Ann Coulter, and Zev, our computer-generated contributor. Al, first of all, let's discuss the issue of ATM fees.

AL FRANKEN: One of these people is computer-generated? Which one? The woman? The black guy?

SOLEDAD: No, the guy in the jester hat.

FRANKEN: Jesus, that's stupid.

SOLEDAD: Okay, so ATM fees. You're opposed to them, right?

FRANKEN: Yes, Soul-dad, is it? I feel that con-sumers pay enough fees of various sorts already—car registration fees, for instance—without having to pay a dollar, or in some cases more, at the ATM.

SOLEDAD: You say "in some cases more." I've never paid more than a dollar. Do some ATMs really charge more?

FRANKEN: Uh, yes. According to Peter Steingarten of the American Enterprise Institute, certain ATMs, typically ones at convenience stores, charge up to two dollars and fifty cents per transaction.

OMAR: Okay, Al, fine. But you're talking about ATMs at convenience stores, not at banks. Is it really fair to blame banks for what these

rogue ATMs, at the 7-Eleven or whatever,
happen to charge?

FRANKEN: Is *he* computer-generated?

SOLEDAD: No. Let's take a question from one of the
bulletin boards on our MSNBC Web site. It reads,
"Is it really fair to blame ba . . ." Okay, it's
pretty much the same as Omar's question.

ANN COULTER: I just think it's so funny to hear
liberals like Al Franken whining about issues like
ATM fees. I mean it's so funny, it just makes me
laugh, I mean it's a riot. Get a life.

ZEV: Don't slip a chip, Ann. Al, let me download
this on you. ATMs are computers. They need lots
of TLC! Just like me! I'll see you on the We-e-e-b!

FRANKEN: So, *he's* computer-generated?

OMAR: Yes, but I think Zev makes a very interesting point. Which is that these fees may be a
good thing.

FRANKEN: With all due respect, Roger, is it? I
don't think you and the robot know what you're
talking about.

ANN: This is the funniest thing I've ever heard.
This is a riot. You liberals think the solution to
everything is more government regulations. It just
cracks me up. I mean, ATM fees. It's hilarious.
What's next?

FRANKEN: I told you. Car reregistration fees.

ANN: That's so funny!

SOLEDAD: I think we've just about exhausted this topic. But you can post a message to Al on our Web site at MSNBC.com. When we return, we'll be asking our contributors their views on what they should be talking about.

May 6, 1999

N made me watch tape of MSNBC appearance five times in a row. Very depressing. Got off on wrong foot with robot. N says not to worry. Fewer than fifty households watching MSNBC yesterday. Also says good practice for future nonrobot interviews. Still can't shake feeling that I have let everyone down. Splurged on hooker.

May 7, 1999

Still depressed. Want to keep hooker for extra day. Both N and J strongly opposed. J asked hooker if she keeps diary. J very worried.

May 8, 1999

Had it with Radio Shed. Got first bill and "special offer" turns out to be complete rip-off. In less than two weeks have racked up over $600 in airtime, plus $60 monthly fee, plus 1 cent for phone, plus $140 "activation fee" that shithead salesman neglected to tell me about. N thinks that cell phone activation fees could be good issue with suburban voters. But seems to me from firsthand observation that N.H. has no suburbs. I hate it here.

May 9, 1999

O called from Arizona or Wyoming. Unclear. Says he lost track of Gore after Iowa. Asked him to come back ASAP to help cheer me up. He said he will try.

May 10, 1999

Unable to get out of bed till almost six P.M. N eventually had to slap me, which made J very nervous. J gave me book, *Chicken Soup for the Soul.* Thought it was piece of shit. As is J. Miss hooker.

May 11, 1999

N has decided that only way to snap me out of depression is to hold big rally in front of ATM machine. Spent day trying to find ATM machine in New Hampshire. No luck so far.

May 12, 1999

Still can't find ATM machine. Finally agreed to ask someone, but he didn't know, either. Beginning to wonder if campaigning on ATM fees in state without ATMs is good strategy.

May 13, 1999

Eureka! Found ATM at candlepin bowling alley in Nashua. Bowling alley manager a total dick. But got phone number of ATM service company off sticker on machine and will call them tomorrow as soon as cell phone batteries finish recharging.

May 14, 1999

We've hit a gold mine! ATM service company says there are four (maybe five) ATMs in N.H. Had to disguise voice so ATM company didn't know it was me. Worked! Nearest one is at outlet center in Puddington Lake. Great ATM and great outlet shopping! Bought ten-pack slightly irregular socks for F and cashmere L.L. Bean sweater for hooker. Big rally planned for tomorrow.

May 15, 1999

Big rally postponed till tomorrow. Not ready yet for big rally.

May 16, 1999

What a day! J and N stayed up all night making signs. "ATM = America's Terrible Menace" and "Don't Bank on ATMs" and J's personal favorite: "Automated $Tealing Machine." Arrived at outlet at noon. Huge crowd already gathered for personal appearance by Dan Haggerty, TV's "Grizzly Adams." Began handing out leaflets written by P in Washington and trying to talk to people about ATMs. Got big boost when hooker showed up with twenty friends from UNH. Had no idea she was a college girl! Even J got into spirit by handing out free hot dogs. After lunch came the speeches, first N, then me, then Dan Haggerty. Turns out he is big opponent of ATMs, for some reason. Says they are controlling the weather. Anyway, he gave rousing speech and local paper took many pictures. My first celebrity endorsement. Then, to top it off, O turned up! With a couple dozen bar friends! I was so excited that I hugged and kissed him and then had to explain to Dan, who thought we were fags. Day ended with big party in outlet center parking lot with me, N, J, O, O's friends, hooker, hooker's friends, N.H. voters, and Dan Haggerty all dancing to off-brand boom box which O "borrowed" from electronics store. O hit Dan Haggerty with board just for laughs and Dan didn't seem to mind. This has been the best day of my life! I'm dancing on air!

May 17, 1999

Very discouraged today. New N.H. poll shows my name recognition well below Gore's despite all we have done. Of people who recognize my name, most have highly negative opinion. But N says this could change.

May 18, 1999

Long debate in car today about whether or not to stay in New Hampshire. O very complimentary about Iowa and N thinks maybe we should go there. Dan also wants to go. No one hates New Hampshire more than me but I made pledge to walk state and don't want to break my word. Could undermine credibility though J says legal. Still, if don't win this time, may run in 2004 when broken pledge could come back to haunt me. What to do?

May 19, 1999

N says Iowa has many more ATMs than N.H. I ask N what about pledge? N says research says that no one in N.H. aware of pledge. I say breaking pledge could come back to haunt me. N says research says it will not come back to haunt me. O and Dan suggested we discuss it over pitcher of beer at Hooters. J refused to come. Fuck him. Got big morale boost when Hooters manager recognized me and said he is big supporter and was not aware of pledge to walk state. Took lots of fun photos with waitresses for Hooters' wall including one of me holding two beer mugs in front of waitress's tits while Dan and O drank from them.

May 20, 1999

Too hung over to decide what to do. Both O and Dan missing. J in complete tizzy.

May 21, 1999

F and kids surprise me for my birthday. So had to cancel party at Hooters. Good to see family, though. Kids agree N.H. is shithole. F says O's ex-wife, Xerina, ("X") looking for him and should she tell her where he is? O says no.

May 22, 1999

F is secret weapon! Visited ten houses with her today. F seemed able to forge bond on human level with S.P. She likes to hear their problems. She says secret is just to listen and not to lecture them about ATM fees.

May 23, 1999

F and I had big fight at church bake sale. She said my contempt for S.P. was too obvious and told me to leave, which I was only too happy to do. F stayed and sold pie to Dan.

May 24, 1999

Picture of F and Dan and pie at church ran on front page of *Manchester Union Leader.* N suggests F stay in state and continue campaign while we go to Iowa. Fine with me since F getting on nerves with criticism of my attitude. Now if only we could leave J behind too.

May 25, 1999

F happy to stay in N.H. but only willing to let me go to Iowa if I take J. Okay, fine. F organized "Farewell, Al" hayride for local underprivileged youth but told me to stay behind at last minute when I made joke about anyone who lives in N.H. being by definition underprivileged. O and Dan big hit on hayride although J insisted Dan too drunk to drive tractor. Watched Cinemax in hotel. *Mary Reilly.* Bad.

May 26, 1999

N brains of outfit. Figured out that even with drop-off fee, would be cheaper to rent car from Alamo than Budget because of unlimited mileage. Also got us one car class upgrade because he is American Airlines frequent flyer. Left old car with F and hit road. O driving with me riding shotgun. N, J, and Dan in back. J in middle, complaining bitterly. Why can't he be good sport like Dan?

May 27, 1999

Massachusetts more fertile ground for ATM message since more ATMs here. Handed out pamphlets at ATM in Worcester. Not much impact because pamphlets have banner heading: "Attention New Hampshire Voters." N caught problem almost immediately. What would we do without N? Watched *Mary Reilly* for second time. Still bad.

May 28, 1999

Got very early start because O unable to sleep due to poor quality methamphetamines he scored from truckers. J says maybe O should not drive but O too wired to ride in back. Compromise by letting O drive. Made good time to upstate NY where people even dumber-looking than in N.H. Dan made funny joke about O getting "speeding" ticket. Not sure if Dan knew it was joke though. Then O got speeding ticket. No joke. State trooper opposed to ATM fees.

May 29, 1999

O promised he would stop taking bad speed and try to sleep last night but seems to have gone to bars with Dan and kept taking speed. Oh, well. J even more jumpy than O. Even N concerned. Says that although O's driving is fast, it is not "accurate" and that we are not following most direct route and that is why we are in Canada.

May 30, 1999

Feels good to be back in U.S. Remember now why I'm running for president. America is great country. Dan insisted we stop in Buffalo for authentic Buffalo wings. Wings good but Dan farting to beat band, stinking up car. J very irritable.

May 31, 1999

N spoke eloquently about the need for campaign finance reform today. He said that unless we reform our campaign finances by spending less we will never make it to Iowa. Agreed that we must all share a room from now on or sleep in car. Dan still very farty. J says no more Buffalo wings. Campaign needs a lift. Plan "minirally" at ATM in Columbus tomorrow.

June 1, 1999

Minirally was disaster. Local drive-time DJ covered it and made dumb cracks. Also, attendance not good despite Dan's presence. Had to buy a bucket of Buffalo wings to cheer everyone up.

June 2, 1999

Now I'm the one that needs cheering up. Spent very uncomfortable night with all five of us crammed into two double beds and cot at so-called Comfort Inn. Some "Comfort." It was more like a "Discomfort" Inn. Wings also a mistake even though Dan in cot. Looked at map and, despite being on road for eight days, are still not very close to Iowa. Maybe time for someone else to drive.

June 3, 1999

A miracle! Turns out J is great driver! Not fast like O but very good at following map to the letter. Go figure. Almost to Iowa. Also, Dan has very nice singing voice.

June 4, 1999

I can practically smell the votes! N says that, if J can maintain average speed of 40 mph, we will be in Iowa by nightfall.

June 5, 1999

Small setback due to disagreement about whether needle on "E" means tank is empty or still 1/8th of tank left to find gas station with cheapest gas. Virtually certain to make it to Iowa tomorrow.

June 6, 1999

Almost there!

June 7, 1999

Iowa, at last! Big hugs all around when we crossed the border.

June 8, 1999

O assumed identity of "Dotto Dranken" first thing this morning and marched around Davenport in big hat handing out flyers announcing my arrival in Iowa. O very proud of flyers featuring clever cartoon he drew himself. While N agrees that pamphlet is very amusing and clever, a simpler way to get publicity is to just call local newspaper. Says they are desperate for stories about something other than corn and soybeans.

June 9, 1999

Quad City Times

CANDIDATE FRANKEN SHARES AGENDA WITH TIMES BOARD DESPITE MISHAP

PLEDGES TO "WALK STATE"

DAVENPORT, IOWA, JUNE 8— Dark horse presidential candidate Al Franken arrived in the Quad Cities area yesterday via motorcade, bringing his own special brand of populism, optimism, and what he likes to call the "politics of the unusual" to Iowa. In a meeting with the editorial board of the *Times,* Franken outlined a broad agenda for "real change for those who need it and no change for those who don't."

The cornerstone of Franken's domestic policy is a plan to eliminate ATM fees in order to "get the banks off the backs of hardworking people such as corn and soybean farmers." Franken, looking alert and relaxed, described his platform during a freewheeling discussion with the editorial board of the *Times* over a luncheon of corn fritters with soy sauce. Also present were Franken's campaign manager, Norman Ornstein, his chief campaign counsel, Joel Kleinbaum, television actor Dan Haggerty, and local booster Dotto Dranken, who expressed constant and highly vocal approval for Franken and his smorgasbord of proposals.

Turning to foreign policy, Franken expressed general support for NATO and the importance of expanding overseas markets for American agricultural products "such as corn and soybeans." When questioned about Iraq, Franken refused to divulge specifics, saying that "prudence demands that any prudent leader of the world's only remaining superpower not limit his options when dealing with a madman such as Saddam Hussein." Franken gave a similar answer when queried about his policies toward China, Bosnia, and Israel. The candidate did stress, however, that he supports a posture of "constructive engagement" on the part of "the world's only remaining superpower" and that he would use America's nuclear arsenal "only as a last resort" when mediating conflicts overseas.

When questioned on a subject close to the hearts of Iowa voters, whether seasonal farm workers should be exempt from certain pro-

(continued on next page)

(continued from previous page) visions of the Workman's Compensation Act, Franken said it wouldn't be prudent to restrict his options on that subject either and then pledged to walk the entire state of Iowa. As campaign manager Ornstein attempted to clarify his candidate's promise, the meeting was interrupted by a disturbance that resulted from Mr. Dranken's giant hat catching on fire. The burning hat, which had been carelessly hung on a wall sconce, was extinguished by the quick-thinking of actor Haggerty, who poured a Michelob beer on it and then threw the smoldering hat out the window, where it landed harmlessly on the head of the statue of town founder Colonel Cyrus Davenport.

Franken cited Haggerty's actions as an example of "the sort of can-do spirit that has made America the world's only remaining superpower."

June 9, 1999

Campaign in uproar. Requires all my diplomatic skills to make peace. N very cross with O. J also cross with O. N explains that O's burning hat prevented him from rescinding my promise to walk state. N brutally frank and says promise unrealistic and curious about why I made promise after terrible experience in N.H. I explain that I am spontaneous and like to act on instinct. N explains that Iowa is three times larger than N.H. and proves it with map. Now I am cross with O.

June 10, 1999

More bad news. O arrested for passing bad check to buy new giant hat. Disagreement about whether to use remaining funds to bail him out. N and J say no. Dan and O say yes. Compromise on no.

June 11, 1999

Magic solution to problem of severely limited campaign finances. Call F in N.H. to wire money. Guess what? F reports significant progress in N.H. Strategy of listening to people's problems and promising to do something about them seems to be working. Food for thought. F reports O's ex, "X," on the warpath. Also, kids having great time in rented cabin on Lake Hugabug. Joe learning to water-ski.

June 12, 1999

O released on own recognizance today after Dan made personal appearance at Wal-Mart, where O passed bad check. O came up with good fund-raising idea while in Davenport lockup. Other candidates have 800 #, why not have "Franken for President" 900 #?

Press 1 to hear Al Franken's views on ATM fees. Press 2 for hot lesbian sex, and so on and so forth. J very opposed, said not "technically" legal. What else is new? N also opposed, but glad someone is thinking about raising money.

June 13, 1999

While O and Dan out researching 900 # idea, I made speech to Elks Club backing out on pledge to walk state. N still not happy. No pleasing this guy! N says he'll write memo explaining clearly his various gripes, beefs, and bitches. Fine, great, let's see it!

FRANKEN FOR PRESIDENT

TO: AL FRANKEN

FROM: NORM ORNSTEIN

DATE: JUNE 14, 1999

RE: HOW YOU CAN STILL WIN

Now that our campaign is entering a new phase, the time seems right for us to assess how far we've come and how far we still have to go. When I agreed to serve as your campaign manager, it was with the full knowledge that you are a newcomer to electoral politics and that your campaign would not be conventional in any sense of the word. Still, without wishing to any extent to dampen your enthusiasm or that of your brother, I believe the time has come to adopt a less-improvised approach that will lead us to victory in November.

Here then are my suggestions for some simple and easy-to-remember guidelines for the future so that we can continue building on the limited progress we have made so far.

1. <u>Learn from past mistakes in order to avoid repeating them in the future.</u> For example: Don't pledge to walk the state as soon as we arrive in a new state. While I appreciate your desire to be spontaneous and act on instinct, you must also be disciplined enough not to promise to do things that are frankly impossible or stupid or both.

2. <u>We need to establish clear and defined roles for each member of your campaign team.</u> As your campaign director,

my responsibilities include defining your platform, determining our schedule, handling all contacts with the media, adjudicating disputes between the various members of your staff, and managing all the other minutiae of the day-to-day operation of the campaign.

Joel, in his role as campaign counsel, will provide advice on the legal underpinnings of our proposed legislative agenda, as well as performing the all-important task of assuring that we comply with all the Byzantine requirements of federal campaign law. Joel also will interface with local law enforcement officials whenever Otto gets into trouble.

Dan is a valuable draw at public events and seems willing to be your unofficial "ambassador" to the Hollywood community. Further, Dan is eager to act as your bodyguard should the need arise.

Otto is your brother and you love him, but I think you will agree that at times he can be a bit of a loose cannon. I propose we give him the title of "Deputy Communications Director" and encourage him to take on the very important job of putting up posters, thereby utilizing his undeniable talent for vandalism and mayhem—not to mention his interest in the graphic arts—to good effect. I further suggest that the campaign adopt a "no beer before sundown" policy for all of its key personnel, including Dan and Otto.

3. <u>From here on out, we must emphasize what works and avoid what doesn't work.</u> Thus far, I have only been able to identify one thing that may be working. The issue of ATM fees, while not perhaps as resonant in New Hampshire as we might have liked, has at least put Al Gore on the defensive. As your brother is so fond of pointing out, Gore has yet to live up to his impulsive (see, you are not the only candidate who may not fully appreciate the

dangers of acting on impulse!) promise to eat his hat and seems unlikely to do so before the primaries.

While it is an impressive accomplishment to have claimed such a popular initiative as your very own this early in the campaign, it is vital that we continue to explore new areas of public concern to avoid being tagged as a "single issue" (ATM fees) candidate. Building on your burgeoning reputation as an expert in banking matters, you might, for instance, come out for (or against) IMF bailouts for corrupt foreign dictators. Or Christmas Club fees. You could oppose them. I'm just spitballing. My colleague Peter Steingarten from the American Enterprise Institute had a suggestion which we should seriously consider. He proposes that we advocate lifting certain antitrust regulations that bar insurance companies from engaging in the lucrative retail banking business. This would encourage greater competition in the banking industry, leading to lower interest rates on mortgages, higher interest rates on savings accounts, and most important, lower fees for such services as ATM transactions.

On the other hand, it is vital that you not dilute whatever message it is that you are trying to get across by using empty catchphrases which it sometimes seems to me that you have picked up unconsciously from the car radio. You may not have noticed it, but during last week's interview with the Quad City Times, you used the phrase "world's only remaining superpower" at least half a dozen times. While it is undeniably true that America is "the world's only remaining superpower," this does not qualify as an "insight" and does not bear repeating over and over and over again.

4. We must put our own financial house in order before we presume to reform the banking sector of "the world's only remaining superpower." Right now we are funding

the campaign from your personal bank account. While this may be a workable approach for a Steve Forbes or a Ross Perot, in your case it is not. Sooner or later we're going to have to raise money from individuals and, yes, business interests.

For example, if we were to follow my friend Peter Steingarten's advice on lifting restrictions on the vertical integration of insurance companies into retail banking, I believe we could count on significant support, both financial and logistical, from major insurance interests.

On the financial side, we can expect *hard* money from the CEOs of companies like Aetna, Travelers, and Prudential, as well as contributions coerced from their underlings. And, barring the unlikely event of substantive campaign finance reform, the potential for *soft* money is virtually unlimited in the form of vicious attack ads against our opponents, which could not be traced back to you personally.

On the logistical side, we would receive not only access to expert macroeconomic analysis and research, but also enough money to pay for a second car, which would put an end once and for all to the never-ending disputes about whether to stop for Buffalo wings or not.

We do not have a full- or even part-time finance director. My suggestion would be to ask Peter Steingarten to see if he can raise some money from some of his insurance friends, which could then be used to hire him to fill that role. I think he may be willing since he has been on thin ice at AEI because of his cozy relationship with the big insurance companies.

Finally, let me repeat the crucial nature of points one and three regarding not repeating costly and time-consuming errors and learning from our mistakes.

Al, in addition to being your campaign manager,
I have the distinct privilege of being your friend. Many
years ago I made a promise to you that if you ever ran
for elective office, I would help you in any way I could.
As Joe's godfather, I have an obligation to your family
to protect you from your own well-intentioned impulses
as well the hostile environment of the rough-and-tumble
political arena.

While I would be less than frank if I didn't say that I
have occasionally been discouraged over the last several
months, I still honestly believe that we have a bright
future <u>if only we could avoid mistakes and learn from the
mistakes we do make</u>.

Yours faithfully,

Norm

June 14, 1999

Got N's memo today but didn't have time to read it.

June 15, 1999

N on my case about whether or not I have read memo. Told him I will get
to it as soon as I can. Too busy getting out and meeting people, which is
really what it's all about, right? O and Dan very stoked about 900 # and
have found some local talent with prior experience and own phone. And
guess what? They're college students! O also wants to set up "Franken
for President" Web site with links to other antibanking and lesbian sex

Web sites. I said fine as long as they keep it between us and don't tell J and N, who seem to get pleasure from pouring cold water on new ideas.

June 16, 1999

Read better part of N's memo today. Congratulated N and told him I think he is doing a great job. Encouraged him to write memos whenever he feels like it. That's why he's here. Think pep talk really raised his spirits.

June 17, 1999

N on warpath because I promised to walk the state again during "Meet the Candidate" event at Methodist Church Community Center. Just couldn't help it. He said this is exactly the kind of thing he was talking about in his memo when he said we must not repeat mistakes. I think I'm going to have to humor N and let him "win this one." Told N that I'll do exactly as he says for the next two weeks as a sort of "experiment."

June 18, 1999

N has crazy idea about getting money from insurance companies in exchange for supporting something they want to do to the banks or something. Great! Fine with me. But why didn't he tell me sooner? Also, N thinks there may be a car in this.

June 19, 1999

We are now officially a two-car campaign! N's friend Peter Steingarten ("P") from AEI arrived today with $. He and N went to N's room to plan intensive two-week whirlwind tour of state. I went to afternoon show of *Disoriented Nymphos* with O and Dan, which was just terrible.

June 20, 1999

N gathered everyone together this morning for what he called a "campaign meeting." It was very cute. He and P had prepared handouts with maps, schedules, etc. Too much to read but then he went through everything using an overhead projector—just like the big guys do! N wants us to leave at sunrise tomorrow and hit Iowa's six largest cities in seven days. Both O and Dan very hungover and not at all enthusiastic but I showed some leadership and came down in favor of N's plan.

June 21, 1999

No sign of Dan and O this morning so we went on ahead without them. J behind the wheel, me shotgun, N and P scheming up a storm in back. When I tell J how unbearably dull Iowa seems to me and how I just want to kill myself and everyone in the state every time I look out the car window, he laughs but says he hopes I'm not still keeping diary. I laugh. Also, one other thing I've noticed: Iowans are really fat.

Got to Des Moines in time for huge lunchtime rally in Equitable Life Plaza with balloons, signs, free bag lunches, and live music from "The ATM Fees Blues Band." Very impressive! I don't know who this "P" is exactly (must remember to read the rest of N's memo sometime) but he sure is pulling his own weight so far!

June 22, 1999

Wow! Ever since P joined campaign, things really looking up. New car with four doors for a change! Rallies with balloons and hot band! And to top it off, after six months of fruitless effort on J's part, P found publisher for my campaign autobiography, *Daring to lead*. Small outfit in Hartford, Conn., by the name of Actuarial Tables Press. Want to print 10 million copies and pay me $650,000 for all rights. Downside is that there will be no royalties from sales because they are not planning to "sell" it, exactly. Will give it to all insurance policy holders in America. But still $650,000 is not bad considering book is not funny like *Rush Limbaugh Is a Big Fat Idiot.*

Day was chock-a-block with events and rallies and all manner of personal appearances. Big screaming crowds. I feel like a rock star, such as Jewel. Too exhausted to write more in diary. But too excited to sleep. Starting to think that it might be a good idea to replace N with P.

TRANSCRIPT OF SPEECH BY AL FRANKEN AT THE ALLSTATE INDUSTRIAL PARK IN CEDAR RAPIDS, IOWA—JUNE 23, 1999

Thank you, everyone! How about a round of applause for LeRoy Jackson and his ATM Fees Blues Band?! Weren't they great? Their first album, *This Is the ATM Fees Blues Band* will be out next month on State Farm Records and you can bet that song "I Got the ATM Fees Blues" will be on it.

My name is Al Franken and I'm running for president. Thank you. And thank you for being here today at the beautiful Allstate Industrial Park here in Cedar Rapids. Isn't this a terrific facility! And remember, you're in good hands with Franken! Wow! Thank you! Wow!

But seriously, you haven't been given the afternoon off work and lunch, a T-shirt, and a free umbrella—that's from Travelers, by the way—no, no, c'mon now, no booing from you Allstate people. Friendly competition is what made this country great.

But I'm not here to talk about friendly competition. No, I'm here to talk about the other kind of competition. Yes, unfriendly competition. The kind of competition that we don't need here in Iowa or anywhere

else in America, for that matter. And who are these
unfair competitors? Yes, I think you've heard of
them. Some of you probably put your hard-earned pay-
check in one just last week. They're called banks.

And what am I talking about? Well, let me tell you
what I'm talking about. I'm talking about ATM
fees! —Thank you, LeRoy. That's a great riff.

Let me get a show of hands here. How many out
there like paying ATM fees? I thought so. Let me
make this very simple. If you like paying ATM fees
and other fees, don't vote for me. I don't want
your vote. Vote for Al Gore. But if you *don't* like
paying ATM fees, there's something you can do
about it. You can vote for a candidate who opposes
ATM fees! That's right. Me!

But I'm not just a single issue candidate. As important as ATM fees are—and believe me, they're
important—there is another, related issue, that is
just as important to every American. It is an issue upon which my opponent, Mr. Gore, has been
suspiciously silent. You know what it is. It is
the un-American restriction on who can and who
can't participate in the retail banking business.
America has been called the Land of Opportunity.
Well, I went to Amsterdam once during a junior
year abroad . . . well, never mind. LeRoy, let's
hear that riff! Great! Okay, let's say one of you
wants to open a retail bank. The government says,
"No, Jim, or Ellen, or José, or Mochtar, you can't
open a retail bank. Why? Because you already own a
large insurance concern." So what?! Who died and
made the government king?

If my campaign is about anything, it is about good old-fashioned all-American fair play. I'm not saying we should subsidize the entry of insurance companies into the retail banking sector. Not a bit! The insurance companies don't need unfair subsidies of the sort that banks get from ATM fees in order to own and operate retail banks. All they need is a level playing field. And what's more American than that?

And I'll tell you one thing. If the insurance companies, companies you know and trust—companies that have been there for you and your family through earthquakes, tornadoes, car accidents, robberies, devastating mud slides, and the death and dismemberment of your loved ones—if these companies are allowed to open retail banks, there's one thing they won't do. That's right. They *won't* charge you a fee for using their ATM! Hit it, LeRoy! All right!

Scientists tell us that the Iowa caucuses are only 193 days away, give or take a day. I promise you that I will be doing everything in my power over the next 193 or so days to ensure that Al Franken becomes the next president of the United States. And all I ask of you, in return, is that you do the same thing. Thank you! Now, let's hear "I Got the ATM Fees Blues" again. LeRoy?!

June 23, 1999

Everyone agrees yesterday's speech huge success. N thinks speech would be even stronger if it was written out word for word instead of me just riffing off his bullet points. N good solid worker, though no P.

June 24, 1999

Four more events today. Prayer breakfast with Gentile clergymen. Must memorize popular Christian prayer: "Our Father," etc. Then another lunchtime rally, this time at Casualty Court, an office and shopping complex in the heart of Sioux City's insurance district. Went okay, but N's speech too technical, particularly section on dampening effect of long bond interest rates on M-2 money supply. However, ATM Fees Blues Band rocked the house as always. Then I was celebrity guest caller at Bingo Bash at senior citizens' center. Tell you one thing. No matter what state you're in, Bingo really brings out the S.P. Finished the day in Des Moines at a reception and dinner with some bigwigs from the insurance industry. Very receptive to my message about deregulating insurance industry. P says raised almost $200,000 in less than hour! P is clearly real wizard at fund-raising.

June 25, 1999

With O and Dan missing, J needed someone to pick on. Settled on new guy, P. Argued all the way from Iowa City to Keokuk about legality of P's fund-raising practices. P says everything on the up and up. N says much "gray area." Fine with me. Spoke to scout jamboree about importance of insurance deregulation. Made joke about how banks should get a special merit badge for fleecing the public. May have gone over their heads. Hey, when I was a kid, I didn't care about insurance deregulation either!

June 26, 1999

Minor setback today when J injured by pig at livestock show. Pig got loose and knocked J over and then began to bite him. J screaming and crying and P, N, and I thought it was pretty funny but J obviously very scared. All of a sudden, guess who turns up? Dan! He picked up pig and threw it back into its pen. The crowd went wild so on balance everything turned out okay, except J has small wound on buttocks and a black eye from where Dan had to punch him to get him to calm down. O back also. Evidently Dan and O have been traveling around Iowa going to livestock shows.

June 27, 1999

The Waterloo Courier

ATTORNEY INJURED BY GIANT HOG

WATERLOO—A New York attorney, Joel Kleinbaum, in Iowa to serve as campaign counsel to longshot presidential candidate Al Franken, was slightly injured today by Petunia, a prizewinning Yorkshire sow owned by Mr. Lyle Stentz, a Moundsview farmer known statewide for breeding enormous swine. Mr. Kleinbaum, who suffered a bite on his buttocks, was treated at the scene by paramedics and Dr. Paul Holmgren, the supervising veterinarian of the Waterloo Livestock Show, and released.

Petunia apparently became enraged by the sound of Kleinbaum's voice, which had been temporarily raised in anger during a discussion with Franken campaign finance director Peter Steingarten. The 314-pound sow burst out of its stall, knocked Kleinbaum to the ground, and proceeded to harass him furiously until removed by TV actor Dan Haggerty (Grizzly Adams) who was visiting the Waterloo area.

(continued on next page)

(continued from previous page)

"I guess she must have known he was a lawyer," joked Stentz, "because I never seen her do anything like that before. Most of the time Petunia, she's a pretty good-natured animal. I sure hope Mr. Klein don't intend to sue her."

Before Mr. Kleinbaum could express his intentions regarding a lawsuit, a settlement was negotiated by Mr. Bruce Anderson, president of Iowa Mutual, the insurer of the annual show, who had just introduced candidate Franken to his fellow judges at the apple pie baking contest.

June 28, 1999

I declared today "Be Nice to J Day." Worked well until midmorning when O showed J Waterloo paper.

June 29, 1999

This has to rank as one of the most exciting days of my life. First thing this morning a truckload of boxes containing shiny new copies of *Daring to Lead* arrived at our motel here in Ames. I gave the very first signed copy to the driver of the truck. The books arrived just in time for our book-signing at the Iowa State U student center sponsored by the preactuarial society of the John Hancock School of Business Administration. Each person requesting an autograph received a free book and an umbrella from Travelers. Place was mobbed with enthusiastic Franken boosters and students trying to get out of rain alike. Dan distracted J with a pig alert while O recruited five new operators for his lesbian phone sex line, which is apparently going great guns. After dinner, read book aloud to campaign "family." Asked N to incorporate funny anecdotes from book into speech, which frankly is a bit dry. Had sex with cutest of new phone operators, who is now asleep.

June 30, 1999

Close call this morning. F phoned at 7:45 A.M. all in a tizzy with cocka-mamie story about saving some old man from drowning. Coed answered phone while half asleep. Guess that's what you should expect from "lesbian" phone operator. By the time I got on, F was mighty suspicious, but I told her coed was campaign volunteer responsible for waking me up. Think F bought it.

July 1, 1999

N wants to know if I know anything about F saving old man's life in N.H. Told him she might have said something about it but explained coed situation, which N grasped immediately. N man of world. N says his wife, Mrs. N, told him story faxed to her by relative who is gay flight attendant (that's another story) for New England Air. Mrs. N faxed to us her fax which came out very blurry. Still, photo definitely seems to be of F. Considering using anecdote about faxing a fax and how blurry it sometimes gets in speech. N had an even better idea. He says that, rather than using faxing a fax anecdote, tell story about F making heroic rescue in speech and play it up big.

The Hugabug Landing Sh🐞pper

CANDIDATE'S WIFE SAVES LOCAL SENIOR

HUGABUG LANDING—The wife of dark horse presidential candidate Al Franken rescued a Hugabug Center man, R. Walter Dillingham, 96, from the swirling waters of Lake Hugabug today. Mr. Dillingham drove his 1985 Oldsmobile Cutlass down a boat landing at the end of Firewood Road in either

Mrs. Franken recounts story of rescue for *Shopper* reporter

an apparent suicide attempt or a driving footwork error.

Hugabug township police chief Ned Ordway theorized that Mr. Dillingham either was depressed or simply forgot that he was driving a vehicle with an automatic transmission and depressed the accelerator thinking it was the clutch. "We see this kind of thing all the time with drivers over ninety," Ordway said.

Mrs. Franken, 46, of New York, who is vacationing and campaigning for her husband in the Hugabug area, noticed Mr. Dillingham driving into the lake at approximately 11:47 A.M. while she was preparing a picnic lunch for her two children, Thomasin, 17, and Joe, 14, and three of their friends, Erin Whitcomb, 16, of

the Townhomes at Hugabug and Benjamin and Nathanial Cobb, both 14, of North Hugabug. Benjamin and Nathanial Cobb are fraternal twins.

After phoning the Hugabug volunteer rescue squad, Mrs. Franken waded into the muddy waters of the lake and attempted to pull Mr. Dillingham through the driver's side window as his car began to sink. After struggling unsuccessfully for several minutes, Mrs. Franken dove repeatedly to the submerged vehicle, which was resting in about eight feet of water, despite being distracted when a canoe piloted by the Cobb twins overturned and began to sink as well.

Eventually, Mrs. Franken man-
(continued on next page)

(continued from previous page)
aged to open the driver's side door and pull the unconscious driver to the surface and then to shore where her daughter, Thomasin, performed CPR.

The first member of the rescue squad to arrive on the scene, Hugabug pharmacist Lee Nickerson, praised Mrs. Franken and her daughter, saying, "There's no doubt in my mind that Mr. Dillingham owes them his life— whatever is left of it."

Dillingham was transported to the Greater Hugabug Memorial Hospital, where he was reported to be in extremely critical condition, suffering from, among other things, a stroke, hypothermia, cancer, and a dislocated left shoulder. "He's in pretty rough shape just now," said hospital spokesman Deirdre Comstock.

Rescue Squad coordinator and local insurance broker Buck Townsend hailed Mrs. Franken as a "hero" and said that "if her husband is anything like she is, he must be quite a fella. He's got my vote and the vote of every Hugabug citizen who cares about water safety. That boat ramp was an accident waiting to happen and we're just lucky that, when it finally did happen, Mrs. Franken was around."

Mrs. Franken was unfazed by her brush with someone else's almost-death. "I just noticed this car driving into the lake and then went in and got him out. I just wish Al, my husband, had been here because he might have been able to pull Mr. Dillingham out without dislocating his shoulder."

Mr. Franken is campaigning in Iowa and, according to a campaign volunteer who answered the phone in his hotel room, was unavailable for comment.

July 2, 1999

Phone ringing off hook! *People, USA Today, Washington Post, Des Moines Register, Manchester Union Leader,* and the other Hugabug paper all phone for my reaction to Franni's exploits. I make joke saying okay with me for Franni to rescue anyone—except Al Gore. Hey, I still got it! Can always go back to comedy!

July 3, 1999

We're back in New Hampshire! P arranged for chartered plane with Aetna executives who were headed to N.H. anyway. That's why legal. Left Dan and O with cars in Des Moines. Fine with them. Big parade tomorrow here in N.H. Me and F honorary grand marshals of Hugabug Center 4th of July parade. *Good Morning America* planning to tape us marching down pathetic main street surrounded by goobers and interview us afterward at firehouse. Great to see kids, although Cobb twins big pains in ass.

July 4, 1999

Tried to convince Joe not to be friends with Cobb twins, who set off firecrackers inside house today. But Joe says he likes them because their dad has motorboat. Maybe so, but they put snake in toilet, giving J big scare. Otherwise, productive day. Sunrise flag-raising ceremony at American Legion Hall, then went back to sleep after having sex with my own little hero. No, not masturbation. F. Parade big joke, but seemed to mean a lot to F to have crowds cheering for her and telling her she is great. Speech went well maybe because summer people are from less stupid parts of the country. *Good Morning America* people wanted shot of F and me visiting old man in hospital but he still in coma. Had to settle for shot of us talking to his daughter, who had large mole with hair growing out of it. Had to use all of my show business training and experience to keep from staring at hairy mole. When we finally got to cabin, F said she wanted to "talk," but I was too tired to do anything but watch TV and make phone calls.

TRANSCRIPT OF SPEECH OF CANDIDATE AL FRANKEN AT HUGABUG MEMORIAL PARK, HUGABUG CENTER, NEW HAMPSHIRE—JULY 4, 1999

Thank you. Thank you. Jesus! What the fuck was that?! The Cobb twins, ladies and gentlemen. Boys,

what say we save the fireworks for tonight? Okay, great. Okay, one more. Great. Thanks, fellas.

Now, you probably know me as Mr. Franni Franken. That's right. It was my wife, Franni, who saved one of your own, Mr. R. Walter Dillingham, from almost certain death last week when he drove his Cutlass into the lake.

I'm here today to rescue you from another sort of death. The death of a thousand cuts from those who would bleed you dry every time you undertake a transaction at an automated teller machine.

In fact, your neighbor Mr. Dillingham told my wife, Franni, as she pulled him out of the swirling waters of Lake Hugabug, that he had been despondent about financial difficulties, including the constant drain of ATM fees, when he made the fateful decision to drive down that boat ramp.

Today is the day when we remember America's heroes. Like our founding fathers, such as George Washington, Thomas Jefferson, and the other ones we remember each time we spend a piece of United States currency. How do you think George Washington would feel if he knew that every time hardworking Americans like Walter Dillingham used an ATM machine, they would be spending one dollar, exactly the type of bill that prominently features a picture of George Washington's face? Well, I don't think George Washington would be very happy about that at all!

And today is also the day we remember our modern American heroes. Like Franni Franken, who risked her own life for that of another, the 96-years-

young R. Walter Dillingham. But Franni's not the
only hero here today. Everyone of you who is 18 or
over can be a hero come primary time by voting for
a candidate who really cares about you. Al Franken.

Thank you. God bless you. May God bless America!

July 5, 1999

F all pissed off this morning. Woke me by banging kitchen cabinets and making big noise with dishes. Told her to be quiet because I haven't been getting much sleep lately (wink, wink—you know why, Diary). Apparently F annoyed by speech because, according to her, Dillingham never said anything about ATM fees and, in fact, never said anything at all. I explained that I thought she said he had. F asked me not to do that again. F has no understanding of politics. Feel we are growing apart.

July 6, 1999

Cobb twins scared shit out of J by putting dead mouse in his mouth while he was taking nap in hammock. Don't much care for Cobb twins, but have to admit J looked funny with tail and legs sticking out. J woke up just when Joe was taking a picture with everyone standing around him pointing at mouse, and screamed blue murder. Told him that's what he gets for sleeping with mouth open.

July 7, 1999

N and P giggling like monkeys about latest poll results. Seems my name recognition has doubled in Iowa and tripled in New Hampshire. Rushed into kitchen and waved poll results in F's face while she was doing dishes. She still maintains that it is wrong to lie, but otherwise happy that campaign is going well. I said her tireless campaigning and saving man's life definitely helped. Then we had sex.

July 8, 1999

P has been busy as beaver. Says Actuarial Tables Press impressed with my success in polls and now wants to pay me royalty of one dollar for each copy they give away. Fine with me! N says we can now afford all-important TV advertising.

July 9, 1999

All-day skull session on TV ad strategy with campaign team except for J, who is in hospital with very bad case of poison ivy. I suggest half-hour bio pic based on my book, directed by Ron Howard or Sir Richard Attenborough, who is very good with historical subject matter. N and P suggest maybe starting with something smaller, such as ad tailored for local market about F's rescue of old man, featuring clips from newspapers and testimonial from Lilibet Dillingham. P says if we add tag about insurance deregulation, ad will "virtually pay for itself."

July 10, 1999

Got first look at storyboards for "Rescue New Hampshire" ad. Very little me. Pointed that out to N and P. Reminded them that I am experienced television performer (the Guy with the Unusually Long Nose Hairs—hello?!) and that the ads should emphasize me, not deemphasize me like the current ads almost seem to do. N and P insist that 30-second ads are unique art form, blah blah blah. I read them the riot act on who's really in charge here, which I think was a little overdue. Told them to go back to their rabbit hutch and I will write script myself.

SCRIPT FOR "RESCUE NEW HAMPSHIRE" CAMPAIGN COMMERCIAL

OPEN ON: HEROIC SHOT OF AL FRANKEN JUXTAPOSED WITH AMERICAN FLAG BLOWING IN WIND

> FRANNI (V.O.)
>
> When I think of courage, I think of my hus-band, Al Franken.

CUT TO: FRANNI IN FRONT OF LAKE

> FRANNI
>
> He taught me a thing or two about having the courage to do what's right. That's why . . .

CUT TO: REENACTMENT OF CUTLASS DRIVING INTO LAKE HUGABUG (STOCK FOOTAGE? MINIATURE?) INTERCUT WITH NEWSPAPER HEADLINE: "CANDIDATE'S WIFE SAVES LOCAL SENIOR"

> FRANNI (V.O.)
>
> . . . when I had to make a split-second de-cision whether or not to dive into Lake Hugabug and rescue a World War II veteran, Walter Dillingham, I didn't hesitate for an instant. I knew my Al was standing right there beside me.

CUT TO: AL IN FLANNEL SHIRT AND JEANS AND HIKING BOOTS. HE WALKS UP TO AND PUTS ARM AROUND FRANNI, WHO'S ALREADY STANDING THERE BY THE LAKE. SHE GAZES AT HIM WITH ADMIRATION.

                          AL
        Hi, I'm Al Franken. And I'm proud of my
        wife, Franni . . .

FRANNI SMILES AND KISSES AL.

                          AL
        . . . for using what I taught her about
        courage when she pulled old Mr. Dillingham
        out of his Cutlass. Now that we Frankens have
        rescued one New Hampshire citizen, we're not
        about to stop until we've rescued everyone in
        New Hampshire from unnecessary and confisca-
        tory ATM fees.

AL THROWS LAUGHING FRANNI INTO LAKE. FREEZE-FRAME.

                     ANNCR. V.O.
        Franken. Bold leadership for the new millennium.

July 11, 1999

Showed N and P my script as helpful example of what good campaign ad would be like. N and P too proud to admit that my script is better than theirs but I know they got the point.

July 12, 1999

One step forward, two steps back. Convinced N and P to do my script by insisting. But now F has an "issue" with it. Does not want to lie about why she jumped into lake. Says she wasn't thinking about me at the time and, besides, when she thinks of courage, she doesn't think of me, she thinks of Helen Keller, if anyone. Says she doesn't want to lie on national TV. Tell her ad is not national, but still no sale. Women!

July 13, 1999

Held auditions for local actress to play my wife in ad. N and P concerned that introducing "fake wife" to American public could bite me on ass. But I explained that I need someone who will just read fucking script and not give me a lot of grief.

July 14, 1999

Disastrous rehearsal with Terri (T). She is not good actress. N and P took me aside to express severe misgivings about T. Took T for walk in woods to explain situation to her. Ended up having sex with her on rotting tree stump. T very good at sex. So what to do?

July 15, 1999

I am genius! Concocted plan to shoot pretend commercial with T then send her home and shoot real version. T is no rocket scientist. Fell for plan and went right home after sex after fake commercial. Think real commercial is a winner with just minor rewrite excising character of "my wife" altogether.

REVISED SCRIPT FOR "RESCUE NEW HAMPSHIRE"
CAMPAIGN COMMERCIAL

OPEN ON: AL STANDING IN FRONT OF WAVING
AMERICAN FLAG

                         AL
        Hello, I'm Al Franken—or as some of you
        may know me: (WITH TWINKLE IN EYE)
        Mr. Franni Franken.

AUDITIONS — July 13

BRANDY — UNABLE TO READ. <u>No</u>

MARY — GOOD READING BUT WEAK CHIN AND WANDERING EYE. MAYBE.

LOUISE — BIG TITS, SEVERE OVERBITE, UNABLE TO READ. MAYBE.

ELLEN — No.

JOANNE — LATE 60'S. TOO OLD? GOOD READING. MAYBE.

WENDY — GAVE ME A BIG ARGUMENT. No.

BRANDY — STILL UNABLE TO READ. STILL No.

VICTORIA — UNABLE TO SWIM. No.

JUSTINE — GOOD READING. BUT ONLY 14. DON'T THINK THIS WILL FLY, EVEN IN NEW HAMPSHIRE. No.

TERRY — FORMER MISS NEW HAMPSHIRE. TERRIBLE READ. BUT VERY SEXY IN A SLUTTY WAY. TOLD HER ROLE CALLS FOR SOME NUDITY. SHE TOOK OFF SHIRT. YES.

CUT TO: NEWSPAPER CLIPPINGS (REAL AND MOCKED-UP)
ABOUT FRANNI'S RESCUE

                        AL (V.O.)
    That's right. My wife, Franni, unselfishly
    risked her own life to save a drowning man,
    New Hampshire resident and World War II
    veteran Walter Dillingham, from the
    treacherous waters of Lake Hugabug.

CUT TO: AL IN FRONT OF LAKE

                        AL
    Our family motto is "courage and modesty"
    and I think my Franni lived up to our
    motto—and then some—when she made that
    heroic rescue and then refused to come
    on this commercial to brag about it.
    But if Franni were here, she'd tell you
    that Walter Dillingham drove into that
    lake because he was despondent over
    unnecessary and confiscatory ATM fees.
    Well, now that we Frankens have rescued
    one New Hampshire citizen, we're not
    about to stop until we've rescued everyone
    in New Hampshire from being robbed every
    time they go to the ATM. Isn't that
    right, Rags?

CUT TO: PHOTOGENIC GOLDEN RETRIEVER BARKING TWICE.

                        AL (V.O.)
    Here, boy!

DOG RUNS OVER TO AL AND LICKS HIM ON FACE. AL
LAUGHS. FREEZE.

```
            ANNOUNCER (V.O.)
  Franken. Here to rescue New Hampshire.
```

FADE OUT

July 16, 1999

Final version of ad much better without T or F there to distract the viewer from me and my message. Told P to buy airtime with some of proceeds from book. Not "technically" legal. P says J, who is still in hospital, will be apeshit when he sees ad. Big laughs all around.

July 17, 1999

Ad premiered last night during repeat of *World's Scariest Police Chases, II.* Couldn't ask for better placement to appeal to feebleminded mouth breathers of N.H.

July 18, 1999

Uh-oh. Today turned out to be a sort of "Be Mean to Al and Give Him Lots of Shit" Day. Felt like I had a "Kick Me" sign on my back. Turned out I did, thanks to Cobb twins, but not the point. Don't know who was madder, F or T. First F gave me static about lies, etc. Yack-yack-yack. Then T called and whined about being replaced by dog. Asked for tape of "original version" with her in it. Told her it was damaged by powerful electromagnet and that's why we had to use dog. Says I could have called. More yack. Told her to not even bother to come over for sex because I was sick of her and F. That shut her up. Then she came over for sex. Then J called from hospital with his panties in a major twist. Couldn't understand what he was saying because he had allergic reaction to penicillin derivative last night and had to have tracheotomy when esophagus swelled. Tried to change subject by discussing scary police chases, especially one where motor home drives down train tracks. J not in mood. "J" is for Jerk.

July 19, 1999

HA-HA-HA. Nyeah-nyeah-nyeah-nyeah-nyeah. Guess whose ad is scoring big with New Hampshirites? Tom Mashberg from the *Boston Herald* phoned to get reaction to new poll results showing Franken now out of single digits and into double digits. Can't do better than double digits. Ha!

TRANSCRIPT OF *THIS WEEK WITH SAM DONALDSON AND COKIE ROBERTS*, JULY 20, 1999

SAM DONALDSON: And finally, George Stephanopoulos, your boy Al Franken has made some surprising headway in New Hampshire. His approval rating in the Granite State is a shocking 87 percent.

COKIE ROBERTS: Well, let's keep that in perspective, Sam. That's largely because of his wife's heroic rescue of a suicidal pensioner. Franken's ads have been playing that up very prominently.

GEORGE STEPHANOPOULOS: Cokie, there's no doubt that Franni Franken is her husband's greatest asset. But give Al Franken his due. He's hit a nerve with the American public on the subject of usurious ATM fees—it's a real sleeper issue. According to statistics compiled by Peter Steingarten of the American Enterprise Institute, the average American uses an ATM machine every three days. That means once every three days the average

American will think about the issue of ATM fees and if Al Franken is successful in linking himself to that issue, they'll be thinking of Al Franken.

SAM: Well, yes, George, but will they be thinking of Franken in a positive way?

STEPHANOPOULOS: Sam, remember how we discussed you not being such an idiot? Franken's whole campaign is about one issue. *Lowering* ATM fees. Do you think people want to pay *higher* ATM fees?

GEORGE F. WILL: Am I the only one who resents the miniaturization of political debate in this country? My goodness! What happened to presidential candidates like William Jennings Bryan, who battled the gold standard with such peerless eloquence?

(PAUSE)

COKIE: Ah yes, what indeed?

(PAUSE)

SAM: Getting back to Al Franken. Is he or is he not a joke? Bill Kristol?

BILL KRISTOL: I think he's a joke, but maybe he's exactly the kind of joke the American people would like to see in the White House for four years.

SAM: Cokie? George? A joke?

GEORGE WILL: Well, if he's a joke, he's a very bad joke. (HOLDS UP *Daring to Lead*) Has anyone else read this? Franken's autobiography? It reads like a

Judith Krantz novel, full of sex and drug use and all manner of despicable behavior. And Franken himself is telling us about it! Disgusting!

SAM: Really, George? Well, I read it and I liked it. I found it refreshingly candid, and I liked the picture on the cover. Can we get a close-up of that?

GEORGE: Sam, stop it. You're just helping him.

COKIE: Well, that's all the time we have. Join us next week when we'll continue our discussion of the quixotic campaign of Al Franken.

GEORGE: No!

CUT TO: DAVID BRINKLEY IN ARMCHAIR

BRINKLEY

For some time now, it's been my privilege to talk to you each week about Depends, the adult diaper I use in order to cope with the embarrassing and oh-so-personal problem of bladder incontinence. This week, I'd like to change the subject a little bit and talk about another embarrassing and very personal problem, one that I, fortunately, do not suffer from—yet—impotence. But someday, if, God forbid, I do become impotent, I am happy to know that the good people at Pfizer Pharmaceuticals have developed a special product just for impotence, called Viagra. I first heard of Viagra from my good friend Bob Dole, who was part of the initial experimental pro-

```
tocol. Bob heard about Viagra from our good
friend Dwayne Andreas, chairman of Archer
Daniels Midland. Is Dwayne Andreas impotent?
I don't know. But if he is, it's probably
because he's under so much stress from trying
to feed a hungry world. Viagra. Helping
Dwayne Andreas feed a hungry world. Cokie?
```

July 21, 1999

P says folks at Aetna very excited about poll results and want to buy another one million copies of book. P and N say we use royalty money to buy more airtime in N.H. and make new ad for Iowa. N says not to discuss with J since doctors say he should be kept calm. T has heart set on part in new ad.

July 22, 1999

Spent day in woods with T writing script for Iowa ad. F wants to know how I got mosquito bites all over ass. Says after full day of campaigning, does not want to come home and put calamine lotion on my hairy butt. Made the kids do it.

July 23, 1999

T loves fake script for Iowa ad. Almost tempted to shoot it with film in camera just to have record, but processing costs money.

SCRIPT FOR "TERRI" CAMPAIGN COMMERCIAL

OPEN ON: SLO-MO OF TERRI RUNNING THROUGH "IOWA"
FIELD (CORN? SOYBEANS?). TERRI IS WEARING TANK TOP.

> ANNOUNCER (V.O.)
> Look at her—young, beautiful, healthy, in the
> prime of life. But over the next fifty years,
> she'll use an ATM machine . . .

AS TERRI RUNS, MONEY FALLS OUT OF HER CLOTHES,
LEAVING HUGE CLOUD OF BILLS TRAILING BEHIND HER.

> ANNOUNCER (V.O.)
> . . . literally tens of thousands of times.
> And every time she uses one, she'll be wast-
> ing money. Money that could be spent on food.

CUT TO: TERRI ABOUT TO BITE INTO SANDWICH—SANDWICH
DISAPPEARS À LA *BEWITCHED.*

> ANNOUNCER (V.O.)
> Or clothes.

TERRI'S CLOTHES DISAPPEAR À LA *BEWITCHED* AND *BASIC
INSTINCT.* TERRI IS NUDE, STALKS OF CORN (?), SOY-
BEANS (?) COVERING HER NIPPLES AND PUBIC HAIR.

> ANNOUNCER (V.O.)
> Vote Franken.

FADE OUT

July 23, 1999

The Franken campaign works hard and plays hard! Had fun day "shooting" commercial with nude T. N was "cameraman." P was combination "soundman" and "makeup artist." Field was full of "soybeans." (Actually pumpkins.) Slight wrinkle when angry farmer arrived, but T (nude) "smoothed things over." Took Polaroids for "Get Well Soon" collage for J in hospital. Sent "film" from shoot to "lab" for "processing." Boy, T is one dumb broad.

July 24, 1999

I will never understand J. Instead of being cheered up by the "Get Well Soon" collage of nude Polaroids of T, he demanded to know if we had a signed model release from her along with a photocopy of her driver's license and an I-9 form confirming that she is a U.S. citizen. Also, J very worried about investigative reporter from *Boston Globe* snooping around hospital for information on exact nature of Walter Dillingham's injuries and reasons for driving into lake. J worried Dillingham may come out of coma and spill beans. Where is O with board when you need him?

July 25, 1999

Great news! O and Dan arrived unexpectedly today. Told O what J said about nosey reporter. He immediately found board and headed to hospital. Dan, meanwhile, became friendly with T. Fine with me, since she was getting on my nerves anyway. Dan also thinks he can repair Dillingham's Cutlass, which is still sitting next to boat ramp. Soon we will be a three-car campaign!

July 26, 1999

O came home last night to assure us that *Boston Globe* reporter now suffering from severe case of "board poisoning." Reporter now sharing room with Gore's guy Bob Squier, who is still experiencing constant nausea and just had a shunt inserted in his skull to drain cerebrospinal fluid. Should have sent the "Get Well Soon" collage to him! O also gave Dillingham a little "lumber massage" for good measure.

July 27, 1999

Time for Franken campaign to hit road again. Kids and F asleep since we left at four A.M. Probably easier that way anyway. Big debate about whether to take J out of hospital. N says we need lawyer more than ever, so Dan smuggled him out of hospital on gurney. Put him in back of Cutlass with morphine drip and sign around neck that says: "Do Not Give Penicillin." Told Dan he could bring T to Iowa if he wanted to, but Dan said not interested.

July 28, 1999

Drive to Iowa good opportunity to brainstorm about what P is calling Phase II of campaign. Should take just five or six days thanks to O's special shortcut using only local roads. Also avoids tolls.

July 29, 1999

Me & P & N have spirited debate. N thinks key to Phase II is refocusing message on core issue: ATM fees. P agrees but thinks we ought to stay "on message" about unfair retail banking restrictions that are strangling the nation's insurance industry. I think time has come to discuss China policy and solution to Bosnia problem. Stopped in Erie to replenish J's morphine drip and clear obstructed windpipe.

July 30, 1999

Took vote in car about what my China policy should be. Even split between "constructive engagement" (N & P) and "nuke the gooks" (O and Dan). J conscious long enough to break tie in favor of N & P. O & Dan could give shit that I didn't go along with their policy ("nuke the gooks"). Nice guys and fun to be around, but not really passionate about the issues like N & P are.

July 31, 1999

Phase II in action! Rally in Indianapolis to celebrate launching of All-state blimp. Blimp trailed big "Franken for President" banner, which got hooked on church steeple. Blimp drove around in circles for a while. We got bored and left.

August 1, 1999

Too hot to continue drive. Spent day at Quality Court pool in Champagne, which is very ironic name for complete shithole. Dan has inexhaustible supply of dirty jokes to help us relax when not brainstorming.

August 2, 1999

Brainstorming pays off big-time with brilliant idea for Iowa campaign commercial. Following N's advice to emphasize what works (finally read N's memo—very interesting) have decided to rescue O as "Dotto Dranken" after he drives car into lake in Iowa.

August 3, 1999

Today J's birthday. Still very ill. Had seizure blowing out candle. Tomorrow, Iowa!

August 4, 1999

Found perfect lake—Hoover Lake, named for President Herbert Hoover, according to sign. N & P alerted local media while Dan and O took dry runs in Cutlass. J highly agitated, but unable to speak, Needs morphine.

TO: NORM ORNSTEIN, PETER STEINGARTEN, JOEL KLEINBAUM, OTTO FRANKEN, AND DAN HAGGERTY

FROM: AL FRANKEN

DATE: AUGUST 4, 1999

RE: HOOVER LAKE RESCUE

NOTE: DESTROY AFTER READING!

Here is the schedule for tomorrow's "event."

> 9:00 A.M. —Breakfast and final briefing at Hampton Inn.

9:50 A.M. —Media arrive at Hoover Lake ATM site for speech by me about ATM fees.

10:00 A.M. —Otto, assisted by Dan, dresses in Dotto Dranken outfit including giant hat.

10:05 A.M. —Norm, Peter, Joel (if able), and I leave Hampton Court for Hoover Lake.

10:06 A.M. —Arrive Hoover Lake.

10:10 A.M. —Begin speech.

10:12 A.M. —"Dotto" leaves Hampton Inn in Cutlass and drives down Shoreline Road. Dan follows in rental.

10:14 A.M. —Dotto turns onto Boat Ramp Lane.

10:15 A.M. —Dotto drives into lake.

10:16 A.M. —I rescue Dotto.

10:16–10:30 A.M. —Dotto and I make statements to press and pose for photos. Dan pulls Cutlass out of lake (if possible) with rental.

P.S. REMEMBER TO DESTROY THIS MEMO AFTER READING!

August 5, 1999

Today's event did not come off exactly as planned. First of all, no one from the press turned up. Unfortunately, O was already en route by the time we arrived, so we figured as long as he was going to drive into the lake, we might as well get a picture of it. P bought disposable camera from lakeside convenience store. Second problem was that O, blinded by giant hat, missed boat ramp and drove off dock instead. Car did not immediately sink and began drifting toward center of lake, with O yelling blue murder because he has always been afraid of deep water. After short discussion with N and P, I took off shirt and posed for picture before diving into lake. Small crowd, (no reporters), had gathered to watch me as I backstroked out to O (Dotto). When I got there the car began to sink, with O getting pretty hysterical. Thank God for O's giant hat, which turned out to be made of some sort of buoyant Styrofoam. Meanwhile, Dan also missed boat ramp and also drove off dock. But he got out of the Nova right away and swam out to us. Good thing he did, because hat was beginning to break up and O was pushing me under. Dan pulled us both into shore and agreed on way in to say that I rescued him. Dan great sport, though he lost Nova.

August 5, 1999

Hoover Lake Shopper

CONFUSING SITUATION AT LAKE

HOOVER LAKE, AUG. 5—A confusing situation developed yesterday morning when dark horse presidential candidate Al Franken, local Franken booster Dotto Dranken, and TV actor Dan "Grizzly Adams" Haggerty were involved in a bizarre multicar accident near the lake's southern end.

According to Franken campaign manager Norman Ornstein, Franken rescued Haggerty and Dranken after both men drove into the lake at approximately the same time to protest high *(continued on next page)*

(continued from previous page)
ATM fees and the exclusion of large insurance companies from the retail banking sector. Ornstein called Franken "a true American hero" who "didn't hesitate to put his life on the line in order to save an Iowan [Dranken] and a beloved TV star [Haggerty]."

Witnesses to the incident described a somewhat different scenario. Henry Bauer, a retired meat wrapper visiting from Keokuk, said it looked to him as though it was Franken who needed the rescuing. "When the big hat began to break up," said Bauer, "I thought for sure those two guys [Franken and Dranken] were goners. Lucky for them the big, hairy guy drove into the lake when he did."

Dranken and Haggerty stood by Franken's version of the story, however, with Dranken even offering to take a polygraph test—an offer that was quickly withdrawn by campaign counsel Joel Kleinbaum.

Lake Hoover police chief Wayne Erickson said that no charges are being filed in connection with the incident nor is an investigation planned. He did say that the registered owners of the sunken cars (the Alamo Rent A Car company and Mr. J. Walter Dillingham of Lake Hugabug, New Hampshire) will be charged for the cost of retrieving the vehicles from the lake bed.

August 7, 1999

Got photos back first thing this morning and couldn't be happier! Picture of O all wet and crazy-looking worth weight in gold. Wrote script over breakfast. Watch out Iowa, here comes my ad!

SCRIPT FOR "THE RESCUE—IOWA" CAMPAIGN COMMERCIAL

OPEN ON: PETER AS LOCAL NEWS ANCHOR. PICTURE OF OTTO AND ME OVER HIS SHOULDER.

> **PETER (AS ANCHOR)**
> Our top story tonight. A local man was rescued from the swirling waters of Hoover Lake this morning by popular Democratic presidential candidate Al Franken.

MUSIC: HEROIC

CUT TO: AL WALKING ON DOCK

                    AL
    Hi. I'm Al Franken. You know, this dock looks
    pretty peaceful. It's hard to believe that
    just yesterday it was the scene of a near
    tragedy caused by . . .

CUT TO: SWISH PAN TO ATM MACHINE

                    AL (V.O.)
    . . . that. An ATM machine.

CUT TO: OTTO ON DOCK

                    OTTO
    Hello, I'm Dotto Dranken, your neighbor.
    My buddy here, Al Franken . . .

WIDEN TO REVEAL AL

                    OTTO
    . . . saved my life in a dark moment when I
    thought I couldn't go on paying high ATM fees.

OTTO PUTS ARM AROUND AL

                    OTTO
    My buddy Al gave me a new reason for hope
    when he told me that he will do everything he
    can when he's elected president, to bring down
    ATM fees and put crooked bankers in jail.

```
                           AL
       You can take that to the bank, Otto.
       Right, Rags?

   CUT TO: A BEAUTIFUL GOLDEN RETRIEVER BARKS TWICE
   AND THEN RUNS ONTO DOCK AND LICKS OTTO AND AL, WHO
   ARE LAUGHING. RAGS JUMPS UP ON OTTO, WHO BEGINS TO
   FALL BACKWARD INTO LAKE. FREEZE.

                      ANNOUNCER (V.O.)
       Franken. Here to rescue Iowa.

   FADE OUT
```

August 8, 1999

O better actor than T. Told P to purchase airtime during *Seinfeld* repeats and Fox special *When Animals Attack Stuntmen IV.*

August 10, 1999

Got together small party in hotel room to watch *When Animals Attack Stuntmen IV.* My ad ran after footage of circus elephant trampling car full of midget clowns. Big argument about whether or not midget clown are technically stuntmen. Trust J to get hung up in technicalities! Anyway, ad big hit. O's "lesbian" phone sex coeds (still bringing in mucho cashola to campaign!) all over me, saying I am television star like George Clooney.

August 11, 1999

P woke me and "lesbian" coeds at crack of dawn with new poll results. Wow! My favorable rating has reached record high, with 67 percent of all respondents saying they have an *extremely* favorable opinion of me, primarily because of my heroic rescue of Dotto and Dan. When asked to characterize their feelings for me, 61 percent said they "love" or "adore" me and when asked which word describes me best, a majority said "hero" or "rescuer." Gore, on the other hand, is described most often as "boring" and "stiff." Still, among likely voters, Gore still leads in all categories except voters who live near water. Gephardt is second, I am a close third, followed by Bradley, then Dotto Dranken, and finally Wellstone, who does lead among black Iowans.

NORMAN J. ORNSTEIN ☉ CAMPAIGN MANAGER

SECRET: PLEASE DESTROY AFTER READING

MEMO: CAPITALIZING ON OUR RECENT SUCCESS

TO: AL FRANKEN

FROM: NORM ORNSTEIN

In recent weeks the campaign has gained extraordinary momentum thanks to a fortuitous series of events coupled with your unique understanding of the power of television. Congratulations.

I will admit that at times I have had doubts about some of your more daring initiatives, such as staging the rescue of your brother Otto. But you overruled me and were right to do so.

However, I would be remiss in my duties if I did not sound a note of caution about certain aspects of the campaign that may come under increased scrutiny now that you have made significant headway in New Hampshire and are coming on strong here in Iowa.

After a conversation with Joel (I didn't go into specifics, but instead posed a series of hypothetical questions to him during one of his recent lucid periods), I have identified the following areas of concern:

1. <u>Very Illegal Activities.</u> Otto's assaults on members of the press, on Gore's campaign team, and on private citizens. The theft of Mr. Dillingham's Cutlass. Wire fraud associated with Otto's phone sex business. The use of proceeds from the fraud to pay for campaign expenses.

2. <u>Illegal Activities.</u> Virtually nonstop patronizing of prostitutes by you and other members of the team. Fraudulent claims in your television advertising. Operating two motor vehicles in a reckless manner. Criminal conspiracy to obstruct justice and engage in interstate flight with respect to your brother's assaults. Skipping out on hotel and restaurant bills in various towns and cities in New Hampshire, Iowa, and in between. The manufacture and sale of highly addictive methamphetamine by members of your campaign team (I didn't know about this either, but Otto spilled the beans last night while high on methamphetamine).

3. <u>Possibly Illegal Activities.</u> The laundering of donations from insurance companies via "royalty payments" for your book. The use of those monies for expenses directly related to your campaign. Failure by the campaign to file timely or accurate financial disclosure forms with the Federal Election Commission. Otto's fraudulent impersonation of "Botto Branken" and "Dotto Dranken."

4. <u>Legal, Though Questionable, Activities.</u> Deceptive claims made during speeches. Dishonest conduct toward your wife and numerous girlfriends. Exaggerated or utterly fictitious account of your own past in book <u>Daring to Lead</u>. And others too numerous to mention.

While all successful modern campaigns inevitably run afoul of arcane federal election laws, I think you'll agree that the above list is unusually long and potentially damaging.

My strong suggestion would be that from this day forward, we attempt to curtail as many of the above activities as possible and that we stop the most serious of them (particularly felonious assaults) altogether.

We're off to a great start, a better start than any of us could reasonably have expected. The lion's share of the credit must go to you, and it is only through your leadership that we can now draw back from the precipice to a safer, more legal campaign environment.

I remain, as always,

Your friend,

Norm

NOTE: <u>DESTROY THIS MEMO AFTER READING!!!!!</u>

August 13, 1999

Took an unusually satisfying shit this morning. It was very large and smooth and shaped like a question mark, even with little dot on bottom. Tried to take Polaroid, but no film left over from shoot with T. Went down hall to get O and Dan to look at it but they had just gone to sleep and didn't want to come and see shit. Also got some sort of memo from N. Looks interesting. Tried to save shit but question mark shape started to deteriorate by lunchtime. Also had to take another shit then. So, everyone will just have to take my word for it.

August 14, 1999

Am sunburnt. Spent entire day on Mississippi riverboat courtesy of P's friends at MetLife. Arrived in Muscatine for big "Franken for Pres." rally, where I received endorsements from Snoopy, Linus, Charlie Brown, and other "Peanuts"/MetLife characters. Interesting mix of insurance types and riverboat gambling supporters on boat. A Mr. Iaconne from Atlantic City made a very compelling case for bringing riverboat gambling to Iowa, which we both agreed is a pretty dull state the way things now stand. Funny thing happened getting onboard boat in Davenport. N and P got into shoving match on gangplank. Something about N's memo (note to self: must read) and money from insurance companies. N fell in river and everyone looked at me expectantly, natch. Fortunately, Dan was able to fish him out with a boat hook.

August 15, 1999

Promised N that if I did not have time to read memo in next few days, I would *make* time!

August 16, 1999

N's memo will have to wait. Got invitation from Conn. state Democratic party to attend "cattle call." All four or five of my fellow candidates will make presentations to Connecticut Dems. N insists I bring F instead of cute "lesbian" coed. P agrees with N.

August 17, 1999

Traveled to Hartford in style aboard the *Annuity,* the flagship of the Geico fleet of executive jets. Very posh, though I sort of wish they hadn't started serving Bloody Marys to O and Dan as soon as we got onboard. Both made long visits to the cockpit en route, though I think Dan may have thought it was the toilet. Big crowd at airport to welcome us, including Snoopy (different Snoopy) and the mayor. Also, tons of press. Made short speech but I was so excited I don't even remember what I said.

August 18, 1999

Apparently what I said at the airport yesterday was very stupid. Or so N tells me. I don't remember. Too excited. But today I was brilliant. First of all, exploited F brilliantly. Made joke about marrying above myself, which won me female vote. She was a great sport and gave very pro-Franken account of the Dillingham rescue. Also, let her and P field majority of questions. They did great. I am so proud. Insurance people really rolled out red carpet. Lots of signs, balloons, even a "We Love Franken" campaign song performed by ATM Fees Blues Band (different one), along with very comprehensive document outlining my positions on everything under the sun.

Spent afternoon meeting reporters and other candidates.
Here are my impressions:

BILL BRADLEY—tall and standoffish. Acts like he's
    king of world.

TOM BROKAW—what a weirdo. Thinks everyone
    is interested in what he has to say.

DICK GEPHEART (sp?)—nice guy. Not presidential material.

AL GORE—what a disappointment! Didn't remember me from
    meeting on highway in New Hampshire. Also standoffish.

PETER JENNINGS—seemed sad and lonely. When I said,
    "Hi," he looked sad and walked away.

BOB KERREY—big head.

BERNARD SHAW—very stupid and pompous.
    Not presidential material either.

DAN RATHER—boy! Everything they say is true.

PAUL WELLSTONE—short. Couldn't stop talking
    about poor people. All right, already. Shut up.

Dinner was huge fund-raiser for DNC chaired by head of insurance PAC.
Thousand dollars a head! Gave speech written by very sharp guys from
insurance think tank. The audience just ate up the technical details about
insurance regulations. Every time I said the words *banks* or *ATM fees,*
they booed loudly. The audience may have even been a bit too partisan
since they were kind of impolite to the other candidates, heckling them
and not really giving them much of a chance to speak. Oh well, that's
what the other guys get for being behind the curve on the issues.

The New York Times

Democratic Hopefuls Make Appearance at Hartford Gathering

HARTFORD, CT., Aug. 18—It's only 10:30 in the morning, but Al Franken has already shaken his 438th hand. Franken, the Minnesota-born author and comedian, has come to Hartford for the quadrennial conclave known as "Conn-Test," convened at the behest of the nation's insurers. Along with fellow Minnesotan Paul Wellstone, former New Jersey senator Bill Bradley, Nebraska senator Bob Kerrey, House Minority Leader Dick Gephardt, and Vice President Al Gore, Franken will spend today and tomorrow meeting with local Democrats, speaking with insurance executives, and participating in a model U.N. with local high school students.

ConnTest has been a major stop on the precampaign tour since John Kennedy broke out of the pack here in 1960 with a speech denying rumors that a secret agreement existed between the Kennedy family and Pope John XXIII to make America a vassal state of the Vatican and committing our armed forces to spreading Catholicism throughout China.

Vice President Gore's media strategist, Bob Squier, who was recently released from a New Hampshire hospital where he has been recovering from a crippling head injury, described ConnTest '99 as "the kind of utterly meaningless event that no serious candidate can afford to miss."

This year's candidates were given an unusually hostile reception by the insurance industry notables, with the exception of Franken, whose message of lower ATM fees and the opening of banking markets to all interested parties including insurance companies has strong appeal here.

During a breakout session on legislative initiatives chaired by Rep. Gephardt, a man in the back asked why the Missouri congressman was "afraid to admit that he was a tool of the banks." When the minority leader denied the charge, the man, Klotto Klanken of Bridgeport, called Gephardt "a bald-faced liar" and asked him why he didn't "just go back to Liar Land?"

Although clearly rattled by Klanken's virtual nonstop harassment, Gephardt said that such criticism "comes with the territory. A vibrant democracy presumes the open exchange of ideas. That's why we're here—I guess," the congressman said afterward.

Outside the hall, Klanken, who describes himself as the owner of a small metal recycling business, said *(continued on next page)*

(continued from previous page)
he "likes what he sees" of candidate Franken. "He's the only one who really cares about the people."

In an unscientific poll conducted in the halls of the Hartford Civic Center, many participants appeared to share Klanken's view, describing Franken as "a fresh face" and as "a guy with some new and exciting ideas." Franken's campaign manager, Norman Ornstein, confirmed that Franken does indeed have many new and exciting ideas and promised to share them with the public at a later date.

In the meantime, Al Gore had also run afoul of Klanken, who confronted the vice president as he was leaving for a private dinner with Connecticut governor John Rowland. "Why are you running away from me?" Klanken yelled at an alarmed Gore. Klanken, who was wearing a giant hat with "Eat Me" written on it in an apparent reference to a statement made by the Vice President in New Hampshire, said that Gore "can run but he can't hide" and that "the Secret Service can't protect [Gore] from the truth."

The event ends tomorrow.

August 19, 1999

Had weird run-in with Gore in hotel elevator last night. He seemed very shook up by angry crowd outside hotel (including O) wearing giant hats and signs that said "Eat Me, Liar Gore." I tried to be sympathetic and suggested him eating hat made of chocolate or marzipan to simply get it over with. Also planted seed of him picking me as running mate in case I don't win nomination by asking him how he likes being VP and whether he thinks I would like it. Gore too shook up to give coherent answer. That's okay. Planted seed.

August 20, 1999

Leaving Hartford on high note as I am winner of straw vote at ConnTest '99. Hors d'oeuvres on insurance company plane cool on outside but very hot on inside due to microwave. Burned roof of mouth. P on phone with riverboat gambling supporters with strong ties to labor in industrial states. P reminds me of Energizer Bunny because he is always energetic in trying to raise money for campaign. Told him this. We all laughed.

TRANSCRIPT OF CNN'S *INSIDE POLITICS*, AUGUST 20, 1999

BERNARD SHAW: And as promised, our own Bill Schneider has "The Play of the Week." Bill?

BILL SCHNEIDER: Bernie, this week's "Play of the Week" was made by Al Franken. Who, you may ask? The Al Franken who came out of nowhere to win a straw poll held at the Connecticut presidential beauty contest called, appropriately enough, "ConnTest." How did the author and comedian pull it off? Well, he's a savvy performer who knows his way around a TV camera. But can an actor really be elected president of the United States? Remember Ronald Reagan? He was an actor too. For *Inside Politics,* I'm Bill Schneider.

BERNARD SHAW: Thank you, Bill. Bill Schneider will be here on *Inside Politics* every Friday with his "Play of the Week." Something to look forward to throughout the coming election year.

August 21, 1999

Time for a little R&R thanks to some of my new riverboat gambling friends. Seems that *they* have some friends in the International Brotherhood of Paperhangers and Pipe Fitters who have a private island in the Bahamas. N & P think I should stay on U.S. soil to capitalize on what they call "surprising" victory in Connecticut. Don't know what they're so surprised about. Need to talk to N & P about concept of loyalty when I return from Bahamas.

September 22, 1999

Excellent four weeks in the sun though hurricanes a constant threat at this time of year due to El Niño. Sunbathing, beach volleyball, and being towed behind motorboat on giant kite every morning great way to get mind off campaign. Though did read first seventy pages of David McCullough's Truman biography and watched part of *Glory* on TNT. The country must never be plunged into civil war again!

September 23, 1999

Tracked N & P down in MetLife building in Des Moines where they have set up temporary campaign headquarters on top floor. Very pretty receptionist recognized me right away and why wouldn't she since there was big picture of me being hugged by Snoopy directly across from her desk. N & P seemed to be working hard when I arrived, but secretary may have tipped them off that I was coming because their offices were suspiciously neat. Anyway, campaign seems to be in great shape with Indian tribes now onboard thanks to tireless efforts of riverboat gambling friends.

September 24, 1999

All-day marathon skull session on state of campaign with N & P and various other people they've hired. Very impressive charts and overhead projector transparencies. But what really caught my eye was special attachment for N's laptop that allows him to project images from his computer directly onto overhead projection screen. If I read the pie charts correctly, money has been pouring in from all sources—not just insurers, riverboat gambling interests, and Indians—since straw poll victory in Hartford.

September 25, 1999

Held first round of interviews with potential additional senior staff members today. Had to make it very clear to N & P that adding new people to team does not mean they are being demoted or that I in any way disapprove of the job they have done. They seem to understand that since it was their idea in the first place.

NOTES FROM STAFF INTERVIEWS

ED ROLLINS — INTERESTING IDEAS ABOUT WINNING SUPPORT
IN INNER CITIES BUT VERY SLEAZY.
USE IDEAS BUT NOT HIM. No.

PAT CADDELL — SAD FACE, LOSER MENTALITY. No.

JAMES CARVILLE — GIVE THAT ACT A REST, BUDDY!
IT'S TIRED. No.

PEGGY NOONAN — COULDN'T UNDERSTAND WHAT THE HELL
SHE WAS TALKING ABOUT OR WHAT SHE
WAS DOING HERE. STRUCK ME AS DESPERATE. No.

DAVID GERGEN — TOO WISHY-WASHY. No.

HAROLD ICKES — HE SCARED ME. AND IF HE SCARES
ME THEN HE'S LIKELY TO SCARE OTHERS. No.

DICK MORRIS — I LIKE HIM! A CAN-DO, GO-GETTING STRAIGHT-SHOOTING, HARD-HITTING, LOOK-YOU-IN-THE-EYE, NO BULLSHIT KIND OF GUY. HE TOLD ME HE WASN'T JUST GOING TO TELL ME WHAT I WANTED TO HEAR. LIKED THAT ABOUT HIM. ALSO TOLD ME I HAVE A GOOD CHANCE OF WINNING. YES.

September 26, 1999

Called F at cabin. Phone disconnected. Suspect Cobb twins.

September 27, 1999

Still unable to reach F. Gave assignment of finding my wife to Morris (here-after "D"). Guess what? D found her right away. F back in New York with kids instead of in New Hampshire campaigning for me. Thanks a lot, F!

September 28, 1999

I feel bad. Chewed F new asshole for abandoning N.H. She explained that kids have several more years of school before they finish and this must be done in New York. When she's right, she's right.

September 29, 1999

D very sympathetic about my blowup with F. D really has what it takes. D is almost like brother to me now, particularly since O is missing and last seen siphoning gas from motorcycle in convenience store parking lot.

September 30, 1999

N & P came to me privately this morning to express severe reservations about D. Told me all sorts of malicious gossip about his private life. Read them riot act. Quoted Bible about Israelites who live in glass houses not casting first stone. N objected to me saying that everyone on the campaign was equally guilty of chasing whores and using employee discount to call lesbian coed phone sex line. N says he has been faithful to wife and only uses phones for business purposes. But that's not really the point, is it, N?

October 1, 1999

Assigned D to work with P and I.I. (insurance industry) on "issue ads" attacking Gore, Gephardt, Bradley, and the rest of my opponents. Told D that ads must be very negative in order to be effective. D way ahead of me.

SCRIPT FOR "WEEPING SNOOPY"
CAMPAIGN COMMERCIAL AD

OPEN ON: SNOOPY DOING "HAPPY DANCE" IN FRONT OF DOGHOUSE TO "PEANUTS" PIANO MUSIC.

CHARLIE BROWN ENTERS WITH EMPTY DOG BOWL.

> CHARLIE BROWN
> Hey, Snoopy, what are you so happy about?

> SNOOPY
> What else, Charlie Brown? It's suppertime!

                    CHARLIE BROWN
Well, that's what I've come to talk to you
about, Snoopy. Gramma and Grampa ate all the
dog food, so there's none left for you.

SNOOPY'S EYES BUG OUT OF HIS HEAD AND HE SPINS
AROUND IN A CIRCLE, RAISING A LARGE DUST CLOUD.

                CHARLIE BROWN (CONTINUED)
Apparently the banks took all their money by
charging excessive ATM fees and now they have
to eat dog food until they die.

                        SNOOPY
But what will I eat?

                    CHARLIE BROWN
Don't ask me. Ask Al Gore.

SNOOPY LOOKS SAD.

                        SNOOPY
Must I starve so Al Gore can get elected?

MUSICAL STING

CUT TO: SNOOPY WEEPING

                    ANNOUNCER (V.O.)
The big banks have already decided who you
should vote for in the year 2000. Al Gore.
Or Dick Gephardt. Or Bill Bradley. Or even
Paul Wellstone. But next year Iowans are going to declare independence from the big
banks. By voting for a candidate who will
tell the banks what they can do with their

```
money. Because this is an issue ad and not
campaign advocacy ad, we can't tell you ex-
actly who that is. But safe to say, it's
none of the above.
```

FADE OUT

October 2, 1999

N thinks D's "Weeping Snoopy" script too "on the nail." D suggests making primitive hand-drawn version of ad at Kinko's and letting focus group decide.

October 3, 1999

Frank Luntz offered to conduct focus group for free. Though he is pollster for Republicans, he is also notoriously desperate starfucker. Will do anything to rub elbows with show business types like me. Frank and D spent day recruiting focus groupers at ATM machines all over city. No blacks. Tomorrow big day.

October 4, 1999

Well! Crow for dinner for N tonight since D's ad tested through roof. Among responses written on cards to image of Snoopy weeping were "profoundly disturbing," "where are these so-called banks and what can I do to stop them?," and "just tell me who to vote for!"

October 5, 1999

The boys are back in town! O and Dan turned up in office this aft with amusing tale of cross-country trip riding in cabin cruiser being towed by truck. Said it is best of both worlds. Made it as far as Grand Canyon before truck driver caught on and kicked them out. Frank Luntz says their story would make a good movie and asked Dan if he wanted to come to Hollywood to pitch it with him. Starfucker!

October 6, 1999

O and Dan off to Korea to supervise animation of "Weeping Snoopy" ad. First class all the way courtesy of the good people at MetLife. J concerned. Told him it was none of his business. J said it was, and we left it at that.

October 7, 1999

D has hired five very swishy homosexuals to attend Gore rallies with signs that say "We're Here, We're Queer, We're for Gore" while chanting, "One, two, three, four, if you're a homo vote for Gore." That's the kind of "outside the box" thinking I've grown to expect from D. D, you're the man!

October 8, 1999

First thing this morning, J burst into my office so angry he could hardly speak. His face was all red and he was sputtering. It was just about the funniest thing I had ever seen. I practically died laughing. I tried to get him to look into a mirror so he could see how ridiculous he looked but J would have none of that. When he calmed down enough for coherent speech, he told me he had read this diary last night. I explained that diaries are meant to be private. But he just got angrier and redder all over again. I guess what happened was that he saw that Brenda (?) Brandy (?), the cute receptionist, was working late typing up the diary and he asked her what she was doing and she spilled beans. You see, Frank Luntz wanted more stories about O and Dan for possible movie pitch in Hollywood. I told him there were plenty of good ones in diary and that's why Brenda (?) Brandy (?) was typing it up, because I have very bad handwriting.

So, long story short, J very upset about diary. And not just negative comments about him. He went through it line by line and I must say it was revelation for me. Realized that campaign has occasionally strayed into questionable areas, at least from strictly legal point of view. Upon reflection, giving diary to Frank Luntz for movie would have been very bad idea. Also, I may have been a little too honest in my assessment of others, including or especially J. It was a good thing J gave me this reality check before diary fell into hands of Republican pollster or Hollywood movie producer such as Peter Guber. Finally, J has earned his keep. Swore to J that I would stop keeping diary once and for all.

November 6, 1999

So much has happened since I stopped keeping diary that I hardly know where to begin. "Queers for Gore" working like charm, terrifying soccer moms throughout state. Some concern, however, on N & P's part that Gore may actually pick up gay vote. D says caucuses being held in Iowa, not Greenwich Village. Typical straight-shooting from D. J a new man since I promised him to stop keeping diary. No point in telling him about gay scheme and bursting his bubble.

TRANSCRIPT FROM *FIVE AT FIVE,*
CHANNEL 5, DES MOINES

CHARLES BUCKNANNON: And finally, the fifth of our five stories on tonight's *Five at Five,* our own Stacey Chase is at the Mason City Raceway where Vice President Al Gore has picked up an unusual endorsement. Stacey?

STACEY CHASE: That's right, Chuck. I'm standing here with Chad Devereaux, the president of Gore's Gay Army, a grassroots group of homosexual supporters of the vice president who have been turning up all over the state whenever Mr. Gore makes an appearance. Chad, why does your group support Gore?

CHAD: We just love him! We love him! We loooooooove Al Gore! (PUCKERS UP AND GIVES KISS TO CAMERA) Woooooooo!

STACEY: Aren't you a little cold out here without your shirt?

CHAD: No, because we're all hot for Al Gore. We're hot! We're burning, baby! Wooooooooo!

CHARLES: Stacey?

STACEY: Yes, Chuck?

CHARLES: Can you ask him whether those pins or rings or whatever they are in his nipples . . . can you ask him whether they hurt?

STACEY: Chad, did you hear the question?

CHAD: Chuck, you're gonna have to come over to my house and find out. Come here, you. Chuck. Chuuuuuck. (BLOWS ANOTHER KISS AT CAMERA)

STACEY: Getting back to Gore, what are some of the issues that Gore's Gay Army is going to be urging the vice president to adopt into his campaign platform?

CHAD: We want him to tell the Boy Scouts to stop discriminating against gay scoutmasters. It's like that song in the musical *La Cage aux Folles*, "You Are What You Are." Anyway, it's like that.

STACEY: I see.

CHUCK: Stacey, isn't the actual title of the song "I Am What I Am"?

CHAD: Oooooooooh!!! Look who knew! Chuuuck! Get her! And you acting all innocent about my nipple rings! I knew I'd met you somewhere before.

STACEY: (CHANGING SUBJECT) Chad, would you like to introduce me to the Gore supporter standing next to you?

(CAMERA REVEALS DRAG QUEEN IN NUN COSTUME STANDING NEXT TO CHAD.)

CHAD: Yes, this is our director of media relations and discipline, Sister Mary Veronica Ejaculata. She loves Gore too.

STACEY: Sister . . . uh, should I call you "Sister"?

SISTER MARY: You can call me whatever you want, sweetie.

(SISTER MARY IS DISTRACTED BY CHAD'S NIPPLE RINGS AND BEGINS PLAYING WITH THEM.)

STACEY: Well, let me ask you both, why is Gore so appealing to your group? What does Gore have that the other candidates, like Al Franken, do not?

(SISTER MARY IS SUCKING CHAD'S NIPPLE
AND UNABLE TO RESPOND.)

CHAD: We love Gore because his entire political
career has been dedicated to fighting for the
rights of people who are outside the mainstream,
who might be considered freaks by some, to live
and work and have parades in close proximity to
quote-unquote "normal" people.

STACEY: And the other candidates? Franken,
for example?

CHAD: Let me just say this to the people of Iowa:
You have a choice to make in the caucuses. You can
vote for a candidate like Al Gore who unabashedly
supports me and Sister Mary and everything we
stand for or you can vote for a guy like Al
Franken who has been very cautious, some might
almost say reluctant, to come out in favor of
nontraditional or extreme lifestyles.

(CHAD AND SISTER MARY BEGIN FRENCH-KISSING.)

CHAD: If Al Franken is elected president even
something as innocent as a French kiss between two
grown men may be officially frowned on, not to
mention such generally accepted practices in the
gay community as golden showers or mummifying your
lover with silver duct tape. Oooooh, there he is!

(CHAD TURNS AND BEGINS WAVING
AT THE VICE PRESIDENT.)

CHAD AND SISTER MARY: Al! Alllllllll! It's us!
We love you! We loooooove you! One-two-three-four,

```
if you're a homo, vote for Gore! One-two-three-
four . . .
```

STACEY: For *Five at Five,* from the Mason City
Raceway . . .

CHAD AND SISTER MARY: . . . if you're a homo, vote
for Gore!

STACEY: . . . this is Stacey Chase with Gore's Gay
Army.

CHAD AND SISTER MARY: Wooooooooooooo!!!!!!!!

CHUCK: Thank you, Stacey. And before we go, I'd
like to say that I've never met Mr. Devereaux. My
wife and I did see *La Cage aux Folles* on a trip to
New York for our fifteenth wedding anniversary, and
the song just stuck in my head. That's all. There's
nothing more to it than that. For *Five at Five,*
this is Charles Bucknannon. We'll see you at ten.

November 8, 1999

N concerned that actors D hired to play "Chad Devereaux" and "Sister Mary Ejaculata" of Gore's Gay Army may be a little over the top. D disagreed so vehemently that he tried to punch N but tripped over an ottoman in my office and fell down. N was thrown off-balance getting out of the way and knocked over a vase full of flowers. The vase hit D on head as did some of the water. It was the funniest fucking thing I ever saw in my life.

November 9, 1999

Decided to get a second opinion about Gore's Gay Army from a disinterested third party: G. Gordon Liddy. Far from the idea's being "over the top," Liddy didn't think it went far enough. Gotta love ol' Gordo. Maybe make place for him in administration as head of security . . . or gay affairs.

November 10, 1999

Met with Leonard (a.k.a. "Chad") and Bernie (a.k.a. "Sister Mary") to discuss Gore's Gay Army. Bernie asking for more money because he's been offered regular job as performer on cruise ship. Also, wants to work in his singing and dancing skills. Fine with me. Checked with G. Gordon. Fine with him too.

November 11, 1999

Funny thing happened today. Don't quite know what to make of it. Airborne Express package arrived from Seoul with tape of "Weeping Snoopy" commercial. It came out pretty good except Snoopy three or four times the size of Charlie Brown. D says we can fix that here. Also, and this is strange part, mysterious note from O inviting me to his wedding to girl whose first or last name is Kim. First of all, O not legally divorced from wife, X. Second of all, O sometimes impulsive and does not think things through. Can't afford to send D, N, or P to Korea. What about J? Yes. J off to Korea.

November 12, 1999

"Franken for President" rallies becoming so routine I almost don't even notice them anymore. Just go where I'm supposed to go, stand where I'm supposed to stand, and hammer away at core message: "ATM fees are too high." D says he has never met a candidate who is as good at staying "on message" as I am. How about that?

November 13, 1999

P poured a little cold water on the campaign today with latest poll results from New Hampshire. Seems I'm slipping a bit without F in state. D suggests creating road company of Gore's Gay Army with all black cast and send to N.H.

November 14, 1999

"Weeping Snoopy" ad to blanket airwaves tonight with multiple runs on *When Animals Attack Cops II.* D had interesting idea on special party to celebrate. Beer bash at "lesbian" coed phone sex headquarters with Gore's Gay Army doing catering.

November 15, 1999

Great party last night. D says even better than parties during Trent Lott campaign. Luntz back from Hollywood to prep media blitz and collect more O and Dan stories for Hollywood pitch.

November 16, 1999

"Weeping Snoopy" ad in heavy rotation, not just airing on Fox anymore. Insurance friends purchased six spots on *Monday Night Football.* Riverboat gambling folks bought three, for total of nine on for Packers–Vikings nail-biter. Luntz research says that almost 41 percent of likely voters have seen the ads and that 98 percent of them describe it as "one of the most memorable ads they've ever seen," along with such classics as "the Budweiser frogs," "the Coca-Cola polar bears," and "the Budweiser lizards."

November 17, 1999

D and Luntz came up with two more powerful scripts for issue ads: "Charlie Brown in Agony" and "The Death of Linus." Sent them off to O and J in Seoul with note to produce them ASAP without squinty Asian eyes this time. Creative tension between Dick and Luntz "camp" and N & P "faction" bearing unexpected fruit. Example: Dick reports Gore's Gay Army drawing actual recruits from hard-core leather daddies and drag queens to Iowa from all over country. Gore, Tipper both visibly upset during recent visit. Chalk one up for D. Meanwhile P has had very interesting preliminary discussion with billionaire Malaysian family who are longtime loyal supporters of Democratic Party. Chalk one up for P!

November 18, 1999

Both factions on my team agree it is time for intensive "media training" session for yours truly. Began by having D, Luntz, N, and P taking turns peppering me with questions on many different issues. Eventually decided it might be better if D, Luntz, N, and P also took turns *answering* the questions while I took notes. Important to be flexible!

NOTES FROM MEDIA TRAINING SESSION

DOMESTIC

1. TAXES — GOVERNMENT BACK WORKING PEOPLE — OFF OF
   N— PAY FAIR SHARE (RICH); FAIRNESS,
   PAYROLL TAXES REGRESSIVE (?) <u>N TALKS TOO FAST</u>

2. SOCIAL SECURITY — IMPORTANT
   BABY BOOMERS - OLDER - GETTING
   LIFE EXPECTANCY — BANKRUPT
   INVEST IN STOCK MARKET - EVERYBODY MILLIONAIRE ?

3. HEALTH CARE — IMPORTANT
   BABY BOOMERS — OLDER - GETTING
   LIFE EXPECTANCY - BANKRUPT

4. ATM FEES — <u>I KNOW THIS ONE !!!</u>

5. MORE HEALTH CARE — PATIENT's BILL OF RIGHTS — <u>FOR</u>
   HMO's - BAD

6. GAMBLING — OK ON RIVERBOATS & INDIAN RESERVATIONS
   REASONS ???
   P TALKS TOO FAST

7. ABORTION — TRAGEDY, AVOID, PAINFUL, DECISION, PAINFUL DECISION, MAN-I, LUNTZ - HOLLYWOOD, LIFE OF THE MOTHER, EXTREMIST— NOT ME, RAPE, INCEST, BOMBING, POPE.

8. GAY MARRIAGE — I'M OPPOSED, EXCEPT IN HAWAII? SANCTITY. BEEN MARRIED 22 YEARS. GOOD PLACE FOR JOKE. GAY MILITARY. ALL GAY MILITARY (??). NO. MILITARY MUST BE MOSTLY STRAIGHT TO FIGHT WAR. ARMY CHAPLAINS NOT PERFORM GAY MARRIAGE.

9. DRUGS — NOT CURRENTLY TAKING. MAJOR SCOURGE. CRIME IN INNER CITIES. GANGS. CRIPS. BLOODS. DRIVE-BY SHOOTINGS. MEXICO, CORRUPT. CAREFUL. HISPANIC VOTE.

10. ENVIRONMENT — IMPORTANT ISSUE — EARTH, CHILDREN, LEGACY, TED DANSON

INTERNATIONAL

★★★★ WORLD'S ONLY REMAINING SUPERPOWER— AL F.

1. TRADE — JOBS, AMERICAN JOBS, $1 BILLION TRADE = ?? JOBS ASK N - TALKS TOO FAST GEPHARDT AGAINST NAFTA. GORE FOR. KEEP STRAIGHT.

2. IMMIGRATION — LEGAL-GOOD ILLEGAL-BAD POTENTIAL SUBJECT TO REVERSE SELF ON. DM - "EL ARMADA DEL GORE ???"

3. RUSSIA-CHINA — CONSTRUCTIVE ENGAGEMENT. TIANANMEN SQUARE - MASSACRE. CHINA - TOO MANY CHINESE. RUSSIA — NOT SUPERPOWER ANYMORE. AMERICA ONLY ONE REMAINING.

4. MILITARY — WORLD'S ONLY REMAINING SUPERPOWER.
　　　BODYBAGS — YOUNG MEN AND WOMEN DON'T WANT TO COME HOME IN.
　　　I DID NOT SERVE, UTMOST RESPECT, MARGINALIZE AS ISSUE.
　　　BASE CLOSINGS — NOT WHERE I AM SPEAKING. NUMBER OF
　　　WARS WE CAN FIGHT AT ONCE — TWO, THOUGH EVEN ONE WAR IS
　　　TOO MANY. FORWARD DEPLOYMENT. 13 CARRIER GROUPS.
　　　WORLD DANGEROUS.
　　　　GOAL: NO WARS DURING MY ADMINISTRATION.

GENERAL AND MISCELLANEOUS

PERSONAL ETHICS — WHITE HOUSE = GLASS HOUSE.
　　　APPOINT FIRST-EVER ETHICS WATCHDOG. BILLY GRAHAM?

CABINET — BEST PEOPLE. NOT NECESSARILY "LOOK LIKE
　　　AMERICA" — MOST OF AMERICA OVERWEIGHT. DIABETES.

OTHER — BROTHER — LOVE HIM DESPITE FAULTS.

CAMPAIGNING TIPS — MAKE EYE CONTACT WITH CROWD.
　　　TOO MUCH EYE CONTACT BAD — LIKE SALESMAN.
　　　REMEMBER NAMES. DON'T USE FIRST NAMES
　　　TOO OFTEN. DALE CARNEGIE.

November 19, 1999

D has booked me on KTLK, "all-drive-talk radio all the time," during the
afternoon block with Bruce Carmody, a very sharp young DJ who is not
like Howard Stern (all this according to D). Good test of new media skills.

**TRANSCRIPT—*THE BRUCE CARMODY SHOW* KTLK,
DES MOINES**

CARMODY: That was The Pretenders, "Back on the
Chain Gang." Here's a guy who's not on the chain
gang. In fact, far from it. He's Al Franken, comedian, author, and now presidential candidate.

FRANKEN: Hi, Bruce. Great to be on your show, Bruce.

CARMODY: Now, I gotta admit, when I first heard
you were running for president, I was thinking,
"This is a joke; this is Pat Paulsen all over
again." But, no, it turns out you're very serious
about this, aren't you?

FRANKEN: Yes, Bruce. You know, there are lots of
issues facing America today, both domestic and
international. On the domestic front, for example,
the issues include everything from taxes to Social
Security, from health care to abortion, gay marriage to drugs, gambling to the environment, such
as protecting our fragile coastal wetlands, and,
of course, ATM fees. On the interna—

CARMODY: Well, let's talk about Social Security
for a second. Everyone agrees the Social Security
system is a mess. What's President Franken going
to do to change it?

FRANKEN: Bruce, I'm going to look you right in the
eye and tell you honestly I don't have all the answers.

CARMODY: Well, that's refreshing. And you are,
in fact, looking me right in the eye.

FRANKEN: Yes, Bruce.

CARMODY: Right. That's enough. Could you stop?

FRANKEN: Sure. But getting back to Social Security, Bruce, we all know that as the Baby Boomers get older, their life expectancy goes up.

CARMODY: I don't follow.

FRANKEN: Huh?

CARMODY: You said "as Baby Boomers get older, their life expectancy goes up."

FRANKEN: Yes. And that's true. See, every year you live, that's a year you didn't die, which, when the year began, was a distinct possibility. Therefore, your life expectancy has increased.

CARMODY: Well, speaking of life expectancy, another reason that people are living longer is better health care. But how are we going to pay for all these sophisticated treatments that keep old people alive?

FRANKEN: Well, I'll tell you one thing, Bruce, HMOs are not the answer. They're really more the problem.

CARMODY: You know, I hear a lot of that.

FRANKEN: Yes, that's why, Bruce, I plan to enact a Patient's Bill of Rights.

CARMODY: Uh-huh. And what would be on that?

FRANKEN: Well, certainly rights protecting patients.

CARMODY: Such as?

FRANKEN: Well, could be anything pretty much . . . X rays.

CARMODY: What about X rays?

FRANKEN: Bruce, what we need is a blue ribbon panel made up not just of doctors but also patients and maybe hospital administrators, but more patients, which would draw up guidelines for a Patient's Bill of Rights, which would protect the patients.

CARMODY: Good idea. What else do we have to look forward to in an Al Franken Administration or decade? I keep thinking of that old bit of yours, the "Al Franken Decade." Very funny.

FRANKEN: Well, Bruce, it was funny, and we had a great time entertaining the folks, but the story of drug use on the show has been greatly over-stated.

CARMODY: See, I didn't bring that up. You brought that up.

FRANKEN: Yes, I did. That's because drugs are a major scourge and lead to crime in the inner cities with the Crips and the Bloods and the like. And a lot of that is coming through Mexico. Nothing against Hispanics, who are very hardworking voters.

CARMODY: Yes, they are. We have many Hispanic listeners.

FRANKEN: Here in Iowa? You're kidding me.

CARMODY: Actually, we're carried all over the country on the Mutual Radio Network. And we also have a Web site.

FRANKEN: That's a good idea. You know, the Internet links Des Moines to Delhi, Cleveland to Calcutta, Boston to Bombay, and Davenport . . . also to Delhi.

CARMODY: Absolutely. We truly are becoming a global world. And as such, the role of president is not just about dealing with domestic issues. A president has to face crises overseas, to lead America on the world stage, so to speak. Would you be able to do that?

FRANKEN: Absolutely, Bruce.

CARMODY: Yes, uh-huh. And for those of you who can't see us, Al is looking me directly in the eye. But what would you do in terms of, say, Israel? You are a Jew, after all.

FRANKEN: Yes, I am. Are you a Jew, Bruce?

CARMODY: No. No, I'm not. I'm a lapsed Catholic.

FRANKEN: Good for you. Now, as far as Israel goes, the first thing we have to do for Israel is to get back all that Nazi gold that is over in Switzerland and return it to its rightful owners. And soon, before the Holocaust survivors are too old to enjoy it.

CARMODY: I'm with you 100 percent. But would you use force to make Switzerland give back the gold? American troops?

FRANKEN: Bruce, although I didn't serve, I have enormous respect for the brave men and women in our military. And the last thing that I would want is for them to come home in body bags. That doesn't do anybody any good. But I think it's important to point out that America is the world's only remaining superpower, and with that comes some responsibility. We have to remember the world is still a very dangerous place. Even a single war is one war too many, but we have to be prepared to fight on two fronts with as many as thirteen carrier groups to maintain our strategy of forward deployment, which has kept us at peace since the end of the second world war and made us the world's only remaining superpower.

CARMODY: So you're in favor of building two new carrier groups? At a cost of almost 15 billion dollars each?

FRANKEN: Huh? What did I say? Thirteen? Uh. It's really up to the experts.

CARMODY: Uh-huh . . . okay, our first caller is Mildred from Pierre, South Dakota. Mildred, how are you, dear?

MILDRED: I'm fine, Bruce. I love your show. And I want to say, Larry King is Jewish, right?

CARMODY: Why, yes, I believe he is.

MILDRED: I thought so.

CARMODY: Do you have a question for Al Franken?

MILDRED: Al, I love you and I think you have a lot of great ideas.

FRANKEN: Thank you, very much. You couldn't move to Iowa for the caucuses, could you?

MILDRED: I could and I will.

CARMODY: How 'bout that? Another voter for Franken. Okay. We have Harmon from right here in Iowa. Otumwa. Harmon, did you get any of those thunderstorms last night?

HARMON: We sure did, Bruce.

CARMODY: Question for Mr. Franken?

HARMON: Yeah, I was watching *Monday Night Football* on, well, I guess it would have been Monday . . .

CARMODY: Great game, by the way.

FRANKEN: Real nail-biter.

HARMON: And I saw an ad where some banks and Al Gore made Snoopy cry. And that really upset my kids. And what I want to know is where are these banks that did this to Snoopy?

FRANKEN: They're everywhere, Harmon, and that's really part of the problem. Let me ask you something, Harmon. Do you have an ATM card?

HARMON: I sure do.

FRANKEN: Harmon, would it shock you to learn that every time you use that ATM card you could be charged a fee that is deducted directly from your bank account?

HARMON: What the . . . ?

FRANKEN: Exactly, Harmon. It could be your savings account, your checking account, an interest-bearing checking account such as a NOW account . . .

HARMON: How about a checking account with overdraft protection?

FRANKEN: Yes. In fact, the banks love those kinds of accounts because they can deduct a fee even when you have a zero or negative balance.

HARMON: Wow. I had no idea. I'm cutting my card up as soon as I get off the phone. But I'm gonna have a little trouble getting my wife's card away from her.

FRANKEN: I hear ya, Harmon. I've been married twenty-two years. And I'm opposed to gay marriage.

CARMODY: Al, I think you may have won another voter there. We've got a caller from right here in Des Moines, Norm. Norm, are you there?

NORM: Yes. Yes, I am.

CARMODY: Norm, how long have you lived in Des Moines? Are you a native?

NORM: I'm just passing through.

CARMODY: Do you have a question for Al Franken?

NORM: More of a comment, really. I just want to
say that whether it's thirteen carrier groups or
fifteen carrier groups, it really doesn't matter.
What's important is that we have a president who
cares about the glorious multihued patchwork quilt
that is the American people and who is willing to
undertake the great project that is American democracy for the coming millennium. We face great
challenges, both ones that are known to us and
ones we cannot hope to know, and I believe that
Al Franken is the right leader for both these
kinds of challenges. America must have someone
with vision, determination, and a fresh perspective, not some weenie technocrat who has all the
facts and figures about numbers of carrier groups
at his fingertips but couldn't lead a turd through
a goose. And I bet the other candidates wouldn't
have known how many carrier groups we have exactly
either. Sorry to get worked up but it's something
I feel passionate about. Godspeed, Al Franken.

CARMODY: Gee. Well, you couldn't ask for a
stronger endorsement than that. Okay, our last
caller is Dotto from Seoul, South Korea. One of
those citizens of the global world we were discussing earlier. Picking us up on Armed Forces
Radio over there, I guess. Dotto, how are you,
buddy? What's going on in soul-ful Seoul?

DOTTO: Al? Al!

CARMODY: Can you turn down your radio, sir? We're
getting terrible feedback.

DOTTO: Al!

CARMODY: Sir, I'm going to have to ask you to turn down your radio.

DOTTO: Al!

CARMODY: Sir? Dotto? Okay, we'll have to let him go. But I want to thank our guest today, Al Franken, who is indeed good enough, smart enough, and doggone it, I like him. Stuart Smiley, there, of course . . .

FRANKEN: Smalley. Smiley was the real person he was based on.

CARMODY: A little Stuart Smalley. We'll see you tomorrow when our guest will be the real person that the Robert DeNiro character in *Awakenings* was based on. Okay, my producer is telling me it's the Robin Williams character. The DeNiro character is a vegetable again, apparently. Good-bye. Drive safe.

FRANKEN: Bye!

November 19, 1999

Everyone agrees that radio appearance was a slam dunk. Had to thank N for pulling me out of the fire on that carrier group thing.

November 20, 1999

No sooner did I decide N is big campaign hero than he starts getting too big for his britches and tells everyone they have to work over Thanksgiving. I had planned to spend holiday either at home with family or in Bahamas with hooker. Either way need to decompress. N says I must build on triumphant radio appearance and remain in state. Told N that the reason for spending Thanksgiving in NY or Bahamas was so I could *give thanks* for not being in fucking Iowa anymore. N said no reason for me to get sarcastic. I said that on the contrary, there was *every* reason for me to get sarcastic because Iowa is like horrible nightmare populated with fat-assed farmers and small-time local nobodies. N said no reason for me to lose my temper. I told him that I had *not* lost my temper, that he had never *seen* me lose my temper, and that if he ever *did* see me lose my temper he would shit his pants and die because he would be so fucking petrified. Then I showed him what it would be like if I lost my temper by trashing hotel room.

November 21, 1999

Asked D to call N to apologize. Also checked with P to see what kind of gift N would like. P suggested picture frame to replace the one with the photo of his family in it that I put fist through when I trashed his room yesterday. Sent secretary (Brandy? Brenda?) out and got him nice one from Pottery Barn for $14. It was silver-plated with gold flower pattern around edge. Not very masculine but still good price.

November 22, 1999

To make N happy and to show him I'm giving 110 percent to campaign have agreed to attend potluck supper at Knights of Columbus Hall tonight even though I hate such things and the S.C. (Stupid Catholics) who attend them. Wrote special speech with jokes just for the Knights.

November 23, 1999

Learned something last night. Kennedy assassination still sore subject among Catholics, at least in Iowa. Told perfectly innocuous after-dinner joke that went like this: "I think we all remember where we were when we first heard that President Kennedy had been shot, thirty-six years ago today. I certainly remember where I was. I was in the Texas School Book Depository." Okay, maybe not world's best joke, but still funny. Have told same joke every Nov. 22nd for more than twenty years and it always gets good laugh. Except last night. Guess big difference between being comedian joking around with Jewish intellectual friends in NY and presidential candidate speaking to goober Catholic church group in Bumfuck, Iowa. Resolve to be more sensitive.

November 24, 1999

Dodged bullet (unlike President Kennedy). No coverage of Kennedy remark and hostile response in Iowa papers. Finalized plans for busy Thanksgiving weekend. Thanks a lot, N. As if I haven't been working hard enough!

November 25, 1999

F and kids arrived today on insurance company plane. Introduced F to D, who took unhealthy interest in her feet. Still gotta admire way he keeps eye on ball.

November 26, 1999

Everybody wants their piece of Al Franken. Joe wants to play ball. Thomasin wants me to help her with term paper on Reconstruction Era. P wants me to read insurance industry briefing book. N wants me to address Grange Hall. D wants F to have pedicure while he watches.

November 27, 1999

Brilliant solution. P played ball with Joe. N helped Thomasin with term paper. F read insurance industry briefing book and then addressed Grange Hall. I had pedicure while watching football game with D.

November 28, 1999

Postpedicure high wore off quickly when faced with needy family and needy campaign team. Beginning to wonder if presidential campaigning is really for me.

Proclamation Of The President Of The United States Of America

WHEREAS I have been empowered by the Constitution and laws of the United States to declare from time to time a national day of thanksgiving . . .

WHEREAS the people of the United States of America have much to be thankful for . . .

WHEREAS it has been a tradition in the United States of America since the earliest days of its founding for people of good-will to come together and share a meal to commemorate a successful harvest . . .

FURTHER that it has been a tradition for this meal to include the rich bounty of our fruitful land and for the participants to include not only members of our own families but also those in need . . .

WHEREAS in the first Thanksgiving the pilgrims and their hosts, the Native Americans, who were here since before recorded time, broke bread together in the spirit of peace, brotherhood, and worshipful community . . .

THEREFORE, I, William Jefferson Clinton, having been elected President by the people of the United States of America do declare that November 25 in the year of our Lord nineteen hundred and ninety-nine is to be a national holiday of Thanksgiving and ask that Americans gather in their homes, schools, community centers, synagogues, and churches and give thanks to Almighty God for the blessings he has bestowed upon them and upon our land.

STATEMENT OF AL FRANKEN, CANDIDATE FOR PRESIDENT, IN RESPONSE TO PRESIDENT CLINTON'S PROCLAMATION OF THANKSGIVING

While I have no doubt that President Clinton, sitting in the splendor of the executive mansion at 1600 Pennsylvania Avenue, has much to be thankful for, I wonder if the rest of us can muster much enthusiasm for such an empty and cynical gesture as the declaration of a national day of "Thanksgiving." To be sure, Mr. Clinton and his cronies have enjoyed a rich bounty from our fruitful land, but what of those among us who must spend this so-called holiday listening to the cries of a hungry child? I humbly suggest that, instead of congratulating ourselves on our own empty good fortune, we take a moment to say a prayer for our fellow citizens who have been forgotten in this frenzy of self-congratulation: those who have been pauperized by confiscatory ATM fees; honest, hardworking insurance company executives who have been denied the freedom of opportunity that is supposedly so cherished by President Clinton and his ilk; and finally, the Native Americans whom our President features so prominently in his politically motivated proclamation.

Dare I suggest that our leader attempt to redress the wrongs of the past by granting the rightful owners of this nation casino gambling licenses so that they can pursue the American dream of financial independence and break free of a cycle of crippling dependency on the barren teat of the Bureau of Indian Affairs? Dare I suggest that he undertake one single meaningful action now in the waning days of his sorry excuse for a presidency? Or must we, American and Native American alike, go like sheep to the slaughter on this sick joke of a holiday? Just asking.

November 30, 1999

Mixed reviews on Thanksgiving counterproclamation. D thinks a little overstated even after I reminded him it was his idea to begin with and that he helped me write it. N thinks anti-Thanksgiving proclamation "risky" even after I showed him favorable response in *Wall Street Journal*. Also, Wellstone sent message of solidarity, trying desperately to grab on to my coattails, since his campaign dead in water. Wellstone not serious candidate according to *Wall Street Journal*.

November 30, 1999

THE WALL STREET JOURNAL

Reasons to Be Thankful

Honest words from politicians are as rare as snowflakes in the Gobi Desert, which is why we were gratified to read presidential candidate Al Franken's passionate state-

(continued on next page)

(continued from previous page) ment issued yesterday in response to President Clinton's hollow pro forma Thanksgiving declaration.

While we disagree with candidate Franken on the matter of ATM fees, we join him in calling for an end to regulation that bars greater competition in the banking industry and outdated blue laws that bar the first Americans, the American Indian tribes, from expanding their efforts to revitalize the once-moribund casino gambling sector.

As Franken rightly points out, Thanksgiving has become more an orgy of national self-congratulation than a time for a truly prayerful giving of thanks and consideration of what each one of us can do to make the world a better place. Perhaps Franken has taken the first step toward returning Thanksgiving to its pre-Revolutionary roots as an affirmation of the miracle of economic bounty won through thrift, hard work, and healthy competition.

One sour note. A political trailblazer like Al Franken is not immune from the deplorable piling-on effect that assails the rare good idea that emerges in the modern political arena. Minnesota senator Paul Wellstone's craven attempt to share credit for Franken's initiative by a callow statement of support reminds us of the old adage that "success has a thousand fathers while failure is an orphan." The true father of this revisionist view of the Thanksgiving holiday is Al Franken, and the sooner a failure-in-the-making like Paul Wellstone acknowledges it, the better.

December 1, 1999

P waltzed in after lunch this afternoon with carry-on luggage. Guess where he was for Thanksgiving? Working, like me? No. P in New York for Thanksgiving dinner at home of big shot brother-in-law who is *Wall Street Journal* editorial page editor. Told N to deal with P. N said he would.

December 2, 1999

Said good-bye to kids, who agree that Iowa is shithole and that I deserve lots of sympathy for being stuck here. F, of course, made many friends during appearances at women's clubs all over state and is planning to stay in touch with pregnant homeless woman she met at soup kitchen. Sometimes I wonder if F and I really compatible.

December 10, 1999

J returned from Korea today with copy of latest ads. Happy to see ad (though think Linus looks too much like Schroeder). Less so J. Particularly because he was bearer of bad news as always. First of all, O not married to Kim. Reason: as J put it, *"She* turned out to be a *he."* Asked J what the hell he meant by that and how a *she* could be a *he* and whether that's the kind of nonsense he learned in law school. But after J showed me Korean newspaper with picture of O on front page being arrested, I now grasp situation. After all, wouldn't be first time O has hit a transvestite with board.

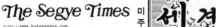

December 11, 1999

Spent day dealing with O crisis. Placed call to State Dept. Got recorded message telling me to press 1 for information on applying for a passport; press 2 for travel advisories for Americans overseas; press 3 for listing of regional state dept. offices, etc. No number to press if brother arrested in foreign country for whacking preoperative transsexual with board. Some reinventing government!

December 12, 1999

Sent J back to Seoul under protest with instructions to either come back with O or not at all. Also to make more commercials while he is there, since new ones are successful. I am now only twelve points behind Gore in latest *Des Moines Register* poll.

December 13, 1999

Learned something last night. Appearing before VFW group told old joke about how fall is like aftermath of nuclear attack on Hiroshima: there's always a nip in the air. Turns out local post commander Ken Nakamura is veteran of 442nd Regimental Combat Team, the famed "Nisei" unit which fought heroically in Battle of Bulge. Took offense. Guess he's hypersensitive like all Japanese. Never too late to learn.

December 14, 1999

Media have descended on Iowa en masse and particularly on Franken campaign. Everyone saying that my recent success is big surprise and Cinderella story. Big surprise to everyone but me.

December 15, 1999

Newsweek has sent ace reporter Howard Fineman to cover me and my own special brand of "post-Perotian" populism. Met with Fineman. No word from Otto.

December 16, 1999

P, N, D, & I have lengthy meeting on how to "spin" Fineman. I say forget spin, let's just tell it like it is. Fineman overhears me saying this, as planned. So N, P, & D's plan working.

December 17, 1999

Tell Fineman there are no secrets from him. He asks about lesbian coed phone line. I tell Fineman I know nothing but that if someone in my campaign has anything to do with it, they will be fired on the spot.

December 18, 1999

Fineman accompanied me to appearance at high school where I spoke movingly about young people, hopes, dreams, aspirations, blah, blah, blah. Later had drinks with Fineman who said that he admired fact that I appeared before high school students who are too young to vote. (Reminder: tear new asshole for moron who booked me at high school.) Fineman had half bottle of Glenlivet and opened up way too much. Seems he is contender for promotion to managing editor, which is Number One Job at *Newsweek*. Fineman worried that "politics" may keep him from getting job. Also Glenlivet.

December 19, 1999

Fineman very embarrassed. Said he can't remember what happened last night. I told him we became good friends.

December 20, 1999

Fineman says *Newsweek* considering cover story on either me or stale topic of search for historical Jesus. Also possible cover on popularity of frozen yogurt.

December 21, 1999

Newsweek goes with historical Jesus cover. Just as well, because Fineman beginning to come around to Franken point of view. Also, caucuses over month away, and Iowans have attention span of mosquito.

December 22, 1999

N says good idea to spend Christmas with family in N.H. Fine with me. Anything to get out of Iowa, even if it means going to N.H.

December 23, 1999

Meet family at Lake Hugabug. Good to be back? D arrived with camera crew and Clio Award–winning commercial director to prepare half-hour live Christmas Eve special: *A Traditional New England Chanukah with the Frankens.* Kids very excited.

A TRADITIONAL NEW ENGLAND CHANUKAH
WITH THE FRANKENS

RUNDOWN

00:01 SHOW OPENS WITH CAROLERS IN FRONT OF FRANKEN
CABIN CAROL: "O LITTLE TOWN OF BETHLEHEM"

01:45 OPENING REMARKS FROM AL IN SWEATER AT FIRE-
PLACE

04:15 AL INTRODUCES GENTILE FRIENDS (COBB FAMILY)
COBB TWINS SING "OH COME ALL YE FAITHFUL"

05:55 COMMERCIAL #1—"WEEPING SNOOPY"

06:30 WELCOME BACK—AL AND FAMILY—LIGHTING OF MENO-
RAH CAROL: "OH HOLY NIGHT"

09:20 FRANNI PREPARES CHRISTMAS AND CHANUKAH COOK-
IES AND INTRODUCES NORM WITH ECONOMIC CHARTS

10:00 PRESENTATION BY NORM CAROL: "DECK THE HALLS"

18:00 COMMERCIAL #2—"THE RESCUE"
(NEW HAMPSHIRE VERSION)

19:00 AL INTRODUCES WALTER DILLINGHAM'S DAUGHTER
SHE ENDORSES AL
PRAYER FOR WALTER DILLINGHAM: LED BY
REVEREND THADDEUS THORNDIKE
CAROL: "DREIDEL, DREIDEL, DREIDEL"

23:00 ROUNDTABLE: REAL MEANING OF CHRISTMAS
AND CHANUKAH (AL, FRANNI, NORM ORNSTEIN,
REVEREND THORNDIKE, DICK MORRIS)
CAROL: "JOY TO THE WORLD"

```
26:00   COMMERCIAL #3—"DEATH OF LINUS"

26:30   SPECIAL PRERECORDED MESSAGE FROM DAN
        HAGGERTY WITH AMERICAN TROOPS AT FIREBASE
        TANGO IN KOREAN DMZ.

27:30   PRESENTATION OF CHANUKAH GELT TO THOMASIN
        AND JOE AND COBB TWINS
        CAROL: "OH CHANUKAH, OH CHANUKAH!"

28:30   FINAL PRAYER (REV. THORNDIKE)

29:00   ENTRANCE OF SANTA (PETER) WHO REQUESTS
        DONATIONS TO CAMPAIGN

29:30   AL GOOD-NIGHTS. ROLL CREDITS OVER PHOTO
        OF WALTER DILLINGHAM
        CAROL: "SILENT NIGHT"
```

December 25, 1999

Christmas always very depressing. Think of Dad and his lawsuits against town for manger display. If he could only see me now, on verge of election to presidency of United States! Realized haven't talked to Mom in over two years. Gave her a call. Not home. Aunt Ruth says that she lives in Florida. Good. Super Tuesday state. Didn't tell her about O and problem in Korea with his being in jail there.

December 26, 1999

Day after Christmas very depressing also. Bad weather. Cooped up with kids and Cobb twins and limited cable system. Saw movie on Bible Channel.

Dec. 27, 1999

Very uplifting talk about last night's Bible Channel movie with Rev. Thorndike, who really knows his shit. Asked him why God would ask Abraham to sacrifice his son Isaac and then stay his hand only at last minute. Seemed unnecessarily cruel thing for God to do. Rev. Thorndike explained that God did not want Abraham to sacrifice his son, just wanted Abraham to prove his obedience to God. Rev says God demands our obedience. Food for thought.

December 28, 1999

Had sex with Terri, who is now married and three months pregnant. Feel guilty. Must be more obedient to God.

December 29, 1999

Very depressed. New poll shows me still trailing Gore despite Chanukah special. Perhaps I have not been obedient enough to God.

December 30, 1999

F out all day, shopping, campaigning, so forth. Terri called to get together. Told her no. That would be disobedient to God. But when she came over, I could not resist and we had sex in coat closet. Why is God torturing me?

December 31, 1999

Am so ashamed of my distasteful behavior that I spent entire day praying.

January 1, 2000

God has answered my prayers! At midnight last night the so-called mil-lennium bug erased billions of dollars in bank accounts of frequent users of ATMs. Otherwise, no effect of bug, which was predicted to confuse computers at start of new century. Ha ha. Only ATM users affected! Out-rage building on Internet, talk radio, and special Jerry Springer.

January 2, 2000

The New York Times

Millennium Bug Attacks ATMs, Spares Rest of Worldwide Computer Network

By GINA KOLATA

MORRISTOWN, N.J., January 1 — The so-called millennium bug, which was widely expected to disrupt com-puter systems all over the world at midnight last night, appears to have left them mostly unscathed, with one notable exception: automated teller machines. As midnight came and went, computer experts watched nervously, fearing such possible con-sequences as the collapse of the air traffic control system, the accidental launch of nuclear weapons, or dis-ruption of the mainframes that con-trol the exchange of securities in the world's markets for capital.

None of that happened. In-stead, the only systems that appear to have been affected are data bases linked to the nation's ATMs. Among the information that appears to have been lost, perhaps forever, is any record of any deposit made at any ATM since the machines came into widespread use in the late 1970s.

Preliminary estimates put the loss at three quarters of a trillion dollars, much of which can be recovered only when ATM customers show some proof of the deposits in question. "We can't simply take their word for it," said Martin B. Reinhold, a beleaguered spokesman for the American Banking Council.

Jane Lefferts, a flight attendant supervisor for Continental Airlines, found herself more than 169,000 dol-lars overdrawn when she tried to with-draw forty dollars from a bank machine in suburban Morristown, New Jersey. "I was shocked," said the 41-year-old mother of two, "because I had never bounced a check in my en-tire life. I am a hardworking American soccer mom who plays by the rules. And now this happens. It's not fair."

(continued on next page)

(continued from previous page)

Peter Steingarten, formerly of the American Enterprise Institute and an expert on retail banking, agrees with Ms. Lefferts. "The sheer arrogance of the major banks and their contempt for ordinary customers like Mrs. Lefferts is a chicken that has been looking for a place to roost. Well, it came home last night. To roost. In spades."

President Clinton expressed sympathy for victims of the banking disaster and said that he was appointing Vice President Al Gore to set up an emergency task force to deal with the problem. "Appointing Al Gore to head up an emergency banking task force is like appointing the fox to guard the henhouse," Steingarten commented.

All of this was slim consolation to Mrs. Lefferts. "I just want my money back," she said, "and if I don't get it, someone will pay."

That someone may well be Vice President Gore, who has been dogged by allegations that he is in the pocket of the big retail banks. Reached in Littleton, New Hampshire, where he is campaigning for president, Gore angrily denied the allegations: "I don't know why people keep saying that. Al Gore cannot be bought."

One of Mr. Gore's opponents, comedian and author Al Franken, who has made ATM fees a central issue of his surprisingly successful campaign for the Democratic nomination, responded to Mr. Gore's statement with barely concealed outrage. "Al Gore can be bought. Al Gore has been bought. And Al Gore has been bought by the big banks. End of story. He knows it; I know it; everyone in Washington knows it; and soon everyone in America will know it. End of story. It was true yesterday; it's true today; and it will be even more true tomorrow. End of story." Franken added, "Appointing Al Gore to head up an emergency banking task force is like appointing the fox to guard the henhouse. End of story."

January 3, 2000

Appeared on all five Sunday morning news shows, tying William Ginsburg's record. My opponent on all five shows was Martin Reinhold, a hapless stooge from some banking industry trade group (who also tied record) who had trouble pronouncing the letter L. I crushed him by making merciless fun of him, not because I think that speech defects and other handicaps are inherently funny but because the banks have stolen so much money from innocent Americans, hundreds of thousands of whom are handicapped themselves!

January 4, 2000

Guess who I saw today? Tom Brokaw! Didn't remember me from Conn-Test. He has even more trouble pronouncing his L's than the stooge from the banking industry. Instead of calling me "Al," he calls me something that sounds sort of like "Arrl." Interviewed me for NBC special on "Nation in Crisis: The ATM Meltdown." Still, you have to wonder what the execs at NBC were thinking when they made him anchor. They really have head up ass when it comes to making important decisions.

January 5, 2000

Family indifferent to ATM crisis. Can't wait for holiday to be over. Kids go back tomorrow. Not a moment too soon. Both F and Terri wanted to meet Tom Brokaw in spite of speech defect. Had to make difficult decision, and in the end chose F because she is official wife. T very cross. Who gives shit? Leaving state soon.

January 6, 2000

D arrived with his "wife" today in N.H. and immediately swung into production of new series of commercials featuring real people telling ATM horror stories. My favorite real person was elderly lady who went to ATM machine to get money for insulin and wound up losing foot.

January 7, 2000

USA Today poll shows Franken soaring, Gore plummeting. *USA Today* editorial cartoon *also* shows Franken soaring, Gore plummeting with big rock labeled "banks" tied around his neck.

January 8, 2000

Never thought I'd be glad to be back in Iowa, but compared to N.H., Iowa seems like Paris. Huge crowd, not just insurance company employees, greeted me at airport, where I made short speech on guess what subject? That's right. ATMs.

TRANSCRIPT OF REMARKS BY PRESIDENTIAL CANDIDATE AL FRANKEN UPON ARRIVAL AT DES MOINES INTERNATIONAL JETPORT

Thank you. Thank you. Thank you, everyone, for coming. And thanks to the band. You know, they used to call themselves "The ATM Fees Blues Band," but after what happened last Thursday, they should be calling themselves "The ATM Millennium Bug Meltdown Blues Band." (LAUGHTER)

When we began this campaign, there were people who said that our key issue, the issue of ATM fees, was not big enough, that it didn't have enough impact on people's daily lives. Well, tell that to Elaine Kyriakis of Bridgeport, Connecticut, who lost her foot! Or tell that to Fiona St. Bartholomew of Aiken, South Carolina, who crashed the ferry boat she was piloting into a bridge pylon because she was not able to get cash to buy a replacement earpiece for her glasses after her dog chewed on them. Twelve people died as a result, and I think if, by some miracle, we were able to ask them whether they think ATM fees are an important issue, their answer would be an unequivocal "Yes, we do." Or tell that to Wendell Bartels of San Diego, California, who inexplicably kept over 4 million dollars in his personal checking account and lost it all last week. Every last

dime. I think Wendell would say that the
hazards associated with ATM fees are pretty
doggone important.

James Carville, whose act frankly is a little
tired, once said that "it's the economy, stupid."
Well, I may not be stupid, but I sure can tell
you that when millions of people lose their life
savings, even temporarily, that's what "it" is.
Economy or not. Tip O'Neill, whose book I read
recently, liked to say that "all politics are
local." Well, put those two sayings together and
I think you have a pretty good summary of the
Franken platform. It's very simple. "All politics
are the local economy, stupid!"

And so, even though the office of president is a
national one, I'm going to start cleaning up the
ATM mess right here in Iowa. And then we're going
to move on to New Hampshire and clean up the ATM
mess there. And one more thing. You know, a couple
days ago Tom Brokaw asked me an interesting question. He said—and I don't do Brokaw, so this will
be a little loose, but it sounded something like
this—"Arrl, who is the one person most responsi-
burrl for the ATM disaster?" And do you know what
I told Tom? I told him that it wasn't fat-cat
banking Brahmins like John Reed of Citicorp, or
even Jon Wetsell, the inventor of the ATM machine.
Oh, they're responsible, all right. But the one
person most responsible for this mess, and I
don't know what else to call it, is Vice President
Albert R. Gore, Jr., or whatever his full name is.
Thank you!

January 10, 2000

I've canceled all appointments in preparation for big debate with me and all my opponents sponsored by League of Lady Voters or some such group. I must say, for the first time I am a bit nervous, doing battle with seasoned politicians on their own turf. Relying on continued obedience to God to see me through.

January 11, 2000

Made important point with N and P today. They brought me 400-page briefing book for debate, which I immediately threw out window in front of them. Don't need 400-page briefing book. Need condensed three- or four-page outline of my positions on all issues. Keep it simple!

January 12, 2000

Stage set for practice debate tomorrow with members of staff standing in for my opponents. N will play Gore. P will play Gephardt. D will play Wellstone. Bradley will play himself. No one to play Kerrey yet.

January 13, 2000

Fortune continues to favor the Franken campaign. Dan Haggerty returned unexpectedly today from South Korea just in time to play role of Bob Kerrey in tonight's mock debate. Dan brought funny pictures of him and O goofing around in South Korean jail. J is in jail too for some reason. What a weirdo! Oh, Bill Bradley canceled. Dan will play him also. After all, he is People's Choice Award–winning actor.

EXCERPT FROM TRANSCRIPT OF PRACTICE DEBATE

NORMAN ORNSTEIN (AL GORE): Bankrupt? I'll tell you who's bankrupt. It's not the banks, who will be making full and timely restitution, with interest, to everyone affected by the ATM crisis. No, the only bankruptcy I'm aware of is that of the Franken campaign, with its platform of stale, rehashed, and thoroughly bankrupt ideas.

AL FRANKEN: Norm, why are you saying that? You came up with my entire platform. And why are you saying "ideas"? We only have one idea. ATM fees. You know that.

ORNSTEIN (GORE): Al, I'm Vice President Gore, remember?

FRANKEN: Oh, right. And, Peter, who are you again?

PETER STEINGARTEN (GEPHARDT): I'm Dick Gephardt.

FRANKEN: Wouldn't it make more sense if Dick was Dick Gephardt?

DICK MORRIS (WELLSTONE): I'm Kerrey.

ORNSTEIN (GORE): No, you're not. You're Wellstone.

MORRIS (WELLSTONE): I am? Since when?

DAN HAGGERTY (BRADLEY AND KERREY): And who am I?

ORNSTEIN (GORE): You're Bradley and Kerrey.

FRANKEN: And I'm . . . ?

ALL: You're you!

FRANKEN: Right.

STEINGARTEN (GEPHARDT): Okay. Let's just start over. Al, why don't you begin?

MORRIS (WELLSTONE): Which Al? Norm or Al?

HAGGERTY (BRADLEY AND KERREY): This is bullshit!

January 14, 2000

Mock debate complete waste of time. Next time make everyone wear signs around necks with name of person who they are supposed to be playing. Or masks. Still need to prepare. Debate important. Decided to watch tapes of old debates with Dan. Dan has good bullshit detector. Made notes.

DEBATE VIEWING NOTES

KENNEDY/NIXON — NIXON- NEEDS SHAVE
KENNEDY - "CU-BER"?

FORD / CARTER — FORD - POLAND, INDEPEDENT; AUTONOMOUS
CARTER- POLAND NOT INDEPENDENT; AUTONOMOUS

CARTER/REAGAN — REAGAN — "ARE YOU BETTER OFF
                         TODAY THAN YOU WERE FOUR YEARS AGO?"
                         CARTER — "DUH?"
                         REAGAN — "THERE YOU GO AGAIN."
                         CARTER — "HUH?"

REAGAN/MONDALE — REAGAN CONFUSED. MONDALE ALSO CONFUSED.

BUSH/DUKAKIS — BUSH — STAY THE COURSE
                    DUKAKIS — KITTY RAPED AND MURDERED

QUAYLE/BENTSEN — BENTSEN — WAS FRIEND OF JACK KENNEDY
                     QUAYLE — FEELINGS HURT

CLINTON/BUSH/PEROT — CLINTON — MOUTH BREATHER
                     BUSH — LOOKS AT WATCH (BAD)
                     PEROT — BOSSY

CLINTON/DOLE — CLINTON — ECONOMY STRONG, NATION AT PEACE
                DOLE — HOLDS PEN

January 15, 2000

Debate tonight at Des Moines Spectrum. Moderator is Jeff Greenfield.
Saw Jeff in lobby of Savery Hotel and told him I used to love him on
Nightline and asked him what he is doing now. He told me he was on
CNN in his trademark nasty and sarcastic way. Didn't know if he was
joking. Hard to tell.

TRANSCRIPT OF *THE NEWSHOUR WITH JIM LEHRER*, PBS—JANUARY 16, 2000

JIM LEHRER: And finally in our news summary, things heated up today along the always tense 38th parallel between the two Koreas, when a man, whom South Korean officials called an escaped convict and North Korean officials called a defecting political prisoner, crossed the demilitarized zone by running through a minefield after pole-vaulting over an electrified fence with the aid of a nearby board. Government officials in both countries and in the United States are said to be watching the situation closely, fearing that even the smallest spark could ignite a regional nuclear conflict in this perennially volatile flash point. That's it for our news summary. Tonight on *The Newshour,* a look at last night's Democratic debate in Iowa. We'll be talking to Shields and Gigot with their analysis. Followed by the third in our seven-part series on the continuing ATM crisis. Then an extended, in-depth look at pay raises for in-home health caregivers in Oakland, California. And finally, commentary from *Newshour* contributor Molly Ivins on why she doesn't use the Internet. But now, Kwame Holman with last night's Democratic debate.

HOLMAN: (IN FRONT OF DES MOINES SPECTRUM) Five men came to Des Moines last night to make their case to Iowa. Al Gore . . .

CLIP OF AL GORE FROM DEBATE: I stand by my record as a key decision maker in the administration that has led this country into an unequaled era of peace and prosperity over the last eight years.

HOLMAN: Bill Bradley . . .

CLIP OF BRADLEY FROM DEBATE: We need a president who can bring Americans together and heal the rifts in our increasingly divided society.

HOLMAN: Dick Gephardt . . .

CLIP OF GEPHARDT FROM DEBATE: I want people in Iowa to get to know Dick Gephardt, and what Dick Gephardt has done for them in the past and can do for them in the future.

HOLMAN: Bob Kerrey . . .

CLIP OF KERREY FROM DEBATE: This election is about courage. Courage to lead. Courage to care. And courage to make the tough decisions that matter.

HOLMAN: Paul Wellstone . . .

CLIP OF WELLSTONE FROM DEBATE: I just don't believe that the richest country in the world can afford to turn its back on its poorest citizens.

HOLMAN: But only one succeeded.

CLIP OF AL FRANKEN: Am I the only one here who is prepared to talk about something that really matters to America: the ATM meltdown? Correct me if I'm wrong, Mr. Vice President, but I think the American people want a leader who can deal with this kind of a crisis, not make it worse, or indeed *cause* it in the first place!

GORE: Now wait a sec—

FRANKEN: No, you wait a second! You caused this crisis. You and your banking buddies, and you know it.

APPLAUSE

GORE: That's not fa—

FRANKEN: No, I'll tell you what isn't fair.
It's not fair to lose your foot!

LOUD APPLAUSE

HOLMAN: Throughout the evening, Franken
focused almost exclusively on ATM fees and the
vice president's ties to banking interests while
the other candidates were left more or less
on the sidelines.

FRANKEN: Let me just ask the vice president
a question. Would you say that you are a man
of your word?

GORE: Yes. Of course.

FRANKEN: And do you believe that a promise is
a sacred trust?

GORE: Yes, look, I think I see where this is
going and I—

FRANKEN: Let me finish! Did you promise a New
Hampshire resident by the name of Botto Branken
to eat your hat if it could be proven that you
had taken campaign donations from banks and—

GORE: Okay, let me clarify that. What I said was—

FRANKEN: What you said was that you would eat
your hat. Don't try to deny it. I brought a hat.
Now eat it!

LOUD APPLAUSE AND CRIES OF "EAT IT!"

GEPHARDT: What about it, Al? Are you going to eat the hat?

GORE: No. And since Mr. Franken brought it up, let's talk about "Mr. Botto Branken" for a minute here.

HOLMAN: And it would be the behavior and identity of this "Botto Branken" that sparked the evening's liveliest exchange.

GORE: Isn't it true that "Botto Branken" of New Hampshire, "Klotto Klanken" of Connecticut, and "Dotto Dranken" of Iowa are all just the same man? Your brother? Otto Franken? Of "No Fixed Address, California"? And isn't it true that he is currently residing in a Korean prison after being convicted of hitting a transvestite prostitute with a board?

LONG SILENCE

JEFF GREENFIELD: Mr. Franken?

AL FRANKEN: My Lord. I didn't think it was possible. Have you and your opposition research sludge mongers sunk so low that you have to come after my brother? My poor defenseless brother? Who sits this very moment in a rat-infested Korean prison for the crime of being a patriotic American? Yes, my brother has had his share of problems. He is a recovering alcoholic and sex addict, and I am proud of him. And yes, I love him. But how dare you? How dare *you* and the banks and your scummy political consultants try to tarnish my good name and the good name of my family with these outrageous lies?

GORE: So you deny that your brother has posed as these three men?

FRANKEN: Yes, I deny it! I deny *categorically* that my brother has ever done anything dishonest on be-half of me or my campaign. But you know what? Let's look at what's really going on here. Al Gore is indulging in the kind of dirty, underhanded, highly personal mudslinging that has turned Ameri-cans off of politics. And I'll tell you one thing. No amount of mudslinging is going to bring back Elaine Kyriakis's foot. But I'm going to do some-thing that can help Elaine. I'm going to take a pledge, right here and now, *not* to stoop to the kind of desperate smear tactics that Al Gore seems to be addicted to. Who here will join me?

WELLSTONE: I will.

GEPHARDT: Sure.

BRADLEY: I've been against smear tactics all along.

KERREY: I will. And let's agree that Al Franken's brother is off-limits.

FRANKEN: Thank you.

APPLAUSE

HOLMAN: It was a stunning performance by Franken as a stunned Al Gore finds himself on the ropes just days before the crucial Iowa caucuses. Kwame Holman, Des Moines.

LEHRER (IN STUDIO): And joining us to put their own spin on last night's debate are syndicated columnist Mark Shields and Paul Gigot of the *Wall Street Journal*. Gentlemen, what happened there?

MARK SHIELDS: What happened there is very simple, Jim. Al Gore self-destructed. I'm beginning to wonder if he's caught the millennium bug himself.

PAUL GIGOT: Well, he did look ill.

SHIELDS: By the end he sure did. He looked awful. All red . . .

GIGOT: Sweaty . . .

SHIELDS: Right, sweaty. And puffy.

GIGOT: Puffy.

LERHER: Paul, is it over for Al Gore?

GIGOT: Maybe not over. Remember, no two-term, sitting vice president has ever been denied his party's nomination. But he certainly didn't do himself any favors with his performance last night.

SHIELDS: Did you see the circles under his eyes? And what was happening with his hair?

GIGOT: Yes, he looked horrible.

LEHRER: Mark, what was Gore's biggest mistake?

SHIELDS: I can put that in two words: Dotto Dranken.

GIGOT: Absolutely. Botto Branken.

LEHRER: So, bad idea to go personal?

SHIELDS: Oh. More than just a bad idea. All of us have someone in our family that we'd rather not talk about. But to go after Al Franken, who frankly is a very decent man, with this sort of lunatic raving. I mean, my God, hitting a trans-vestite with a board? What was Gore smoking when he came up with that?

GIGOT: Well, I hate to agree with Mark, but Otto Franken may very well be remembered as Al Gore's Waterloo.

LEHRER: Uh-huh. Now, I'm going to ask a question that I never thought I'd hear myself asking. Can Al Franken be elected president of the United States?

GIGOT: Jim, he's smart. He's dedicated. He cares passionately about ordinary people. And he's put together a highly disciplined campaign team on a shoestring budget. I think he could go all the way.

SHIELDS: I have to agree with Paul. We all knew Clinton's heir apparent was a guy named Al. It just may turn out that it's Al Franken.

LEHRER: As opposed to Al Gore?

SHIELDS: Yes.

GIGOT: I agree.

LEHRER: Let me ask you one more thing. If you two
are going to agree on everything, why do we bother
to have two of you on the show?

MUSIC: *NEWSHOUR* STING

January 16, 2000

Frank Luntz arrived early today in A.M. because I am star and he is
desperate starfucker. He and D planning to blanket airwaves with ad
composed of footage from debate of Gore looking red and puffy and
refusing to take pledge. Press jammed into lobby begging for interviews. Must hire good press secretary since Brenda? Brandy? frankly
not up to job. Cannot fire her because she is black woman.

January 17, 2000

Tough day. Howard Fineman of *Newsweek* confronted me this morning
with incriminating clipping from *Lake Hoover Shopper* about botched
lake rescue with photo of "Dotto." Agreed that "Dotto" does bear strik-
ing resemblance to Otto, but told him I had to attend an urgent rally and
bolted. Hope he doesn't figure out connection with lesbian coed phone
sex line because I know he uses it often. Beginning to wonder if financing campaign through lesbian coed phone sex line is worth the risk.

January 18, 2000

N had private talk with Howard Fineman, Jew to Jew. N told him it would
be a "schande for the goyim" if Howard printed article with photos
comparing Otto with "Dotto." Fineman said, "Tell that to Admiral
Boorda," evidently referring to Jewish Navy chief of staff who shot himself to death just before article appeared in *Newsweek* questioning his
right to wear certain military medals. N tried to buy time by offering ex-

clusive interview with real "Dotto Dranken," but told Fineman that it may take a couple months to find him. Fineman said he will go with story in three days, interview or no interview, and will release evidence to *Newsweek* editors when he delivers finished article.

January 19, 2000

Emergency session on the "Howard Problem." Dan suggested a "Final Solution." Thought it would be ironic if Otto, about whom Howard has been digging dirt, were the one to actually kill him—with the use of his trademark board. The last thing Howard would see would be Otto swinging the board at his head so he would die knowing he was right about his suspicions.

Told everyone we must not resort to "magical thinking" and fantasize about having Howard murdered. That simply isn't practical. But still no solution. N says Howard's article will be finished in two days.

January 20, 2000

Saved by bell. P's sources in media tell him that Howard is being passed over for top job at *Newsweek*. P has a plan.

January 21, 2000

I scheduled an early meeting with Howard this morning and we all took turns working on him from different angles. I was "Good Cop," N was "Bad Cop," P was "Rich Cop," Frank Luntz was "Focus Group Cop," and Dan was "Scary, Psychotic Cop." I began by opening up to him and coming clean on full Otto story. Told him I know what it's like to experience a major disappointment. In my case, it was my brother. I also told him about my lifelong ambition to one day be president. Asked him what his ambition was and then it all came pouring out. Howard unbelievably bitter about being passed over in favor of Jon Alter, whom he called a "worm" and an "asshole licker." Howard said Alter "never reported anything outside his office." Then N came in and threatened to ruin Howard if he ran article. I told N that we didn't need a "Bad Cop" anymore because Howard had caved and were ready to move right on to "Rich Cop." P worked his own special breed of magic by offering Howard job of Press Secretary at a salary of $550,000 per year. I sweetened the pot by offering to let him fire his predecessor (Brandy? Brenda?). Luntz baffled everyone when he came in and started doing his "Focus Group Cop" routine, but that could be because we were halfway through the bottle of Glenlivet by then. Of course, we had forgotten about Dan, and no one told him not to burst in and start beating shit out of Howard. Howard was good sport about it all and said he didn't feel the blows hardly at all. We all finally managed to convince Dan to stop. So happy ending. Welcome aboard, Howard!

Newsweek

$2.95

The Front Runner

Franken leaves Gore in the dust

The Front Runner

W hen it was all over, Al Gore's bewildered team scrambled to pick up the pieces of his shattered campaign. Some were in denial. "I don't think it was that bad," said Gore media consultant Bob Squier.

"If Bob Squier thinks that, he's suffering from permanent brain damage," said Jeff Greenfield, who witnessed the debacle from the moderator's chair.

Others seemed stunned. "There's a lot of dust in the air right now," said longtime Gore consigliere Jack Quinn. "We're hoping that when it settles, our man will still be on top."

But a few seemed to have come to terms with the fact that Gore's campaign was over even before it began.

"We're dead, d-e-a-d, dead," said a Gore insider who refused to be named. "You know how dead we are? Dead dead."

The vice president himself was not commenting officially. But those who have seen him in the days since the debates describe a man who has watched a future

that he believed was guaranteed to him almost by birthright slip away before his very eyes.

"He's like the only survivor of a horrible plane crash," said one observer, "who wishes he had died along with everybody else. Moments from that debate will be going through Al Gore's mind forever."

6:30 A.M. FRANKEN WORKS OUT AND WORKS THE PHONE. THREE PAPERS AND FIVE MILES TO GO.

And powerful images they were. An indignant Al Franken accusing the vice president of stooping to a new low in the sorry history of gutter politics. A wily Al Franken rubbing Gore's nose in his own questionable relationship with big banks. A professorial Al Franken with facts and figures at his fingertips. A compassionate Al Franken challenging Gore to repair the amputated foot of a diabetic Connecticut woman (see box). In the end, Gore, looking tired and puffy, could only stand and watch as all four of his opponents humiliated him by taking a pledge not to use tactics Franken had called "desperate and sleazy."

Franken, who played an unlikely David to Gore's lumbering Goliath, was understandably jubilant following the debate. "I always knew we'd do it," said a generous Al Franken, sharing credit for his stunning performance with his guerilla campaign team, which operates out of a modest suite of borrowed offices in the MetLife tower in downtown Des Moines.

The crowd at the Des Moines Spectrum seemed enraptured by the magic man of the moment. "There he is! I got his picture!" shouted Mona Thousingbolt of Iowa City as she reached out to try to touch the passing candidate, as if hoping some of his miraculous powers would rub off on her. Thousingbolt, who

had never heard of Franken before Monday's debate and had been a regional chairperson for the Gore campaign, now said she will "do everything I can to make sure that Al Franken is elected president and that poor woman gets her foot back" (see box).

Although Franken seemed to many to have come out of nowhere, canny political handicappers inside the Beltway have been watching his campaign with interest for some time. "Franken has got it all," said a former fellow of one of Washington's most prestigious think tanks. "He's got the will; he's got the guts; he's got the smarts. And now, he's got the momentum."

Where did this Cinderella story begin? Forty-seven years ago in a small, hardworking town called Christhaven, Minnesota, where a shopkeeper, Herman Franken, taught his son, Alan, that he could be anything he wanted to be, except a member of the Christhaven Country Club, which did not admit Jews then or now.

And indeed, Franken has become anything he wanted to be in his short forty-seven years, be it an Emmy-winning television writer, a best-selling author, or a counselor and advisor to presidents, prime ministers, and corporate leaders. But why would a man as successful as Al Franken leave the lucrative world of public speaking for

the bruising realpolitik of a race for the White House?

"I need the money!" says Franken, displaying the trademark wit that has made him one of the best-loved comedians of this or any generation. "And you know why I need the money? Because I use ATM machines," he said, topping his first joke with an even better one.

But the notorious cash machines are more than a source of good-natured fun for the curly-haired wonder boy, they are one of the central issues, perhaps *the* central issue, of the Franken agenda, and, as such, deadly serious. While some may see the recent ATM meltdown as merely a lucky coincidence for the candidate, he himself saw it as a train waiting for a place to crash. "When you start taking money from people, something like this is bound to happen sooner or later." In fact, Al Franken has been way ahead of the curve on the ATM issue, warning of their peril for months, well before the January 1 systemwide failure.

In capturing the moral and intellectual high ground on issues like ATMs, retail banking regulations, and Indian casino gambling, Franken shows all the razor-sharp populist reflexes of a seasoned political veteran. But no one who spends a day or two around the rough-and-tumble Franken campaign would confuse it with politics as usual. "He defi-

The Foot Heard 'Round the World

On January 1st when Elaine Kyriakis set out from her home in Bridgeport, Connecticut, she little suspected that she was about to become the most famous victim of the nationwide ATM meltdown. After stopping at a convenience store to buy Lotto tickets, a bottle of black cherry soda, and a bag of M&Ms, Ms. Kyriakis, who has suffered from type I diabetes melitus since 1987, drove to the local branch of the Chase Bank. "I could feel myself slipping into insulin shock as I pulled up to the drive-through ATM. I knew I needed some cash fast so I could buy some insulin."

But another type of shock awaited the 67-year-old former coffee shop waitress at the Chemical ATM. "Instead of a positive balance of 647 dollars from my social security, it showed a negative bal-ance of over 37,000 dollars and shredded my card. I was very upset."

But the trials and tribulations of Elaine Kyriakis were just beginning. After driving to a drugstore and being turned down when she asked for some free insulin, she drove to another drugstore, where she was again refused free insulin. While driving to a third drug store, Mrs. Kyriakis ran out of gas. By the time a state trooper found her, he could see just by looking that her foot was in serious trouble.

"I didn't like the look of her foot one bit," said trooper Tommy McDonnell, "and I knew we had to get Mrs. Kyriakis and her foot to a hospital stat." Doctors at the Mercy Hospital Foot Center tried to detach and then reattach Mrs. Kyriakis's foot in an unsuccessful attempt to restore normal circulation.

Word of Mrs. Kyriakis's plight spread rapidly. "We heard about millions of people losing their life savings when the ATM computer system went down, but here's a woman who suffered a more tangible loss—in the form of her foot—and it helped the public put a human face on the story," said media watcher Kathleen Hall Jamieson of the Annenberg School of Communications at the University of Pennsylvania. Jamieson counted over twelve thousand mentions of Mrs. Kyriakis and her lost foot in stories relating to the ATM crisis and twelve additional mentions in articles about the relationship between diabetes and obesity.

Mrs. Kyriakis owes much of her emergence into the media spotlight to presidential candidate Al Franken (see story), who featured her time and time again in speeches and in a series of highly effective and aesthetically beautiful ads produced by media wizard Dick Morris.

Mrs. Kyriakis had a chance to thank Franken personally after he arranged to have her MEDEVAC-ed to a campaign rally in Dubuque. "Everybody gave me a big cheer when Mr. Morris wheeled me out onto the stage," Mrs. Kyriakis said, her eyes welling with emotion. "I'll miss my foot, but having the privilege of meeting and voting for Al Franken almost makes up for it."

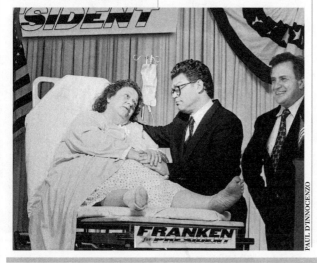

PAUL D'INNOCENZO

FRANKEN WITH FRANK LUNTZ. NO POLLSTERS AT VALLEY FORGE.

nitely likes to think outside the box, to color outside the lines. And we like to encourage him, because that's where many of his best ideas come from," said Franken's energetic campaign manager Norman Ornstein, whose enthusiastic "gee-whiz" style is infectious.

Franken's daily whirlwind campaign schedule would exhaust a man half his age. At 6:30 A.M. Franken has already been up for several hours and is in the middle of a ten-mile run on his treadmill while reading the last of the six newspapers his voracious mind devours each day and giving an interview to an East Coast talk radio program on his cell phone.

At 8:00 A.M. Franken convenes a daily briefing. Surrounded by aides and assistants, he is clearly in

**TWELVE NOON—FRANKEN AND TRIBAL LEADERS.
GREEK SALAD AND BULL SESSION**

command and in his element displaying his legendary attention to detail, whether it be the spelling of *diabetes* on a press release or the menu for an upcoming information-gathering dinner with senior economists from the insurance industry.

By ten o'clock, Franken, who keeps a strict health regimen and limits himself to a mere 1500 calories a day, is munching on a multigrain wafer while reviewing the latest research data with pollster Frank Luntz.

2:45 P.M. TEAM FRANKEN ON THE ROAD AGAIN.
"DON'T CUT ANYONE OFF WITH AN IOWA LICENSE PLATE."

Showing a rare flash of temper during a heated exchange with Luntz over the role political expediency will play in his still evolving campaign, Franken asks rhetorically, "Did George Washington take a poll before Valley Forge? No, he didn't. End of story."

During lunch, Franken maintains an open-door policy, watched over by loyal secretary and gatekeeper Brenda Jackson, welcoming petitioners from all walks of life to these informal bull sessions. Today he is sharing his usual repast of a Greek salad, iced tea, and a carrot with members of a local Indian tribe. Franken clearly feels their pain, not in a sanctimonious and artificially showy way like Bill Clinton does, but sincerely, honestly, and privately. "We owe these people a debt that has not been fully discharged and can never be repaid by a mere apology," he says, clearly moved by their story of alcoholism and neglect by Federal gaming officials.

1:30 P.M. Franken's modest motorcade, comprised of a rented Ford Explorer, a borrowed Chevrolet Caprice, and media advisor Dick Morris's Lexus, begins the three-and-a-half-hour journey to downstate Keokuk. Franken will spend the time strategizing with his team, working the cell phone until the battery gives out, and closing his eyes for some

...he is clearly in command and in his element displaying his legendary attention to detail...

PAUL D'INNOCENZO

5:03 P.M. RAISING THE ROOF AT HILL HIGH. "IT'S HIM! IT'S HIM!"

quiet meditation whenever it is not his turn to drive.

At five o'clock Franken juggernaut arrives in Keokuk for a "Meet the Candidate" event at Ham-burger Hill Memorial High School. The atmosphere is electric as Franken enters the packed gymnasium, so much so that Franken jokes, "When I came in here, I thought I had accidentally walked in on a Cougars pep rally," bringing down the house before his speech has even begun. Unlike every other presidential candidate since the Civil War, Franken has no set stump speech and tailors his remarks individually for each appearance. Tonight the subject is to be the urgent need for banking reform, manna to the ears on the heads of the people gathered at Hill High.

A lone dissenter rises to heckle Franken during the Q&A session that follows by peppering him with questions about his position on gun control. Avoiding a canned, rote response, Franken almost appears to be inventing his policy right there on the spot. To ham-

mer home his opposition to private ownership of semiautomatic assault weapons, Franken pulls a chilling rabbit out of his intellectual hat. "If I had a machine gun, I could kill each and every one of you in just a few seconds," Franken tells the crowd, which at first lets out a collective gasp, then applauds, and then finally rises to a standing ovation in acknowledgment of the potency of Franken's graphic hypothetical.

After the speech, Franken seeks out the heckler, who would give his name only as "Waco Pete," for a few

words in private. "Though I don't like his stand on gun control," "Pete" said later, "I liked what he had to say about the threat posed by banks, and he seemed interested in what I had to tell him about the dangers of the electrical fields generated by high tension power lines."

Ornstein, who never ceases to be awed by his boss's ability to forge a bond with ordinary citizens on a one-on-one basis, smiles and remarks, "I just wish Al could talk to every person in the United States individually—the way he tried to do in New Hampshire. It's just impossible not to like him."

10:45 P.M. Back in Des Moines after a long drive during which his superior night vision proves to be a lifesaver, Franken makes the most important call of the day: to his wife, Franni, and kids, Joe and Thomasin. "Family isn't just a *part* of Al Franken's life, it *is* his life," says senior advisor Dick Morris.

Indeed, family is not just a part of the Franken campaign, it *is* the Franken campaign, as Dick Morris might say, so much so in fact that his campaign staff refers to themselves simply as "The Family." And like every family, the Franken family and the Franken campaign family have their troubled members, and in both cases it is Al Franken's brother Otto, a sweet-souled recovering alcoholic and sex addict, who is currently imprisoned in Pyongyang, North Korea.

6:38 P.M. FRANKEN MEETS "WACO PETE."
"IT'S IMPOSSIBLE NOT TO LIKE HIM."

"I'm basically a very simple guy. I get up at four in the morning, I work hard, love my family, and I demand as much from others as I do from myself."

And thereby hangs a tale of the dirty politics of dirty laundry gone awry. At last Monday's debate, Al Gore sought to tarnish Franken's hard-won image as a political "Mr. Clean" by claiming that Otto Franken had impersonated several other men, all of whom have made trouble for the vice president at various points during his ill-fated campaign. Gore seemed so sure of his facts when he charged during the debate that Otto Franken, Botto Branken, Dotto Dranken, and Flotto Flanken were all one and the same person that Al

Franken seemed momentarily taken aback.

Gore's low blow backfired almost instantaneously, though, when Franken, his voice choked with emotion, categorically denied the charges (which an exhaustive NEWSWEEK investigation found to be totally baseless) and then challenged Gore to give up this game of dirty pool forever by pledging to declare the candidates' families off-limits during the upcoming election. As millions of Americans watched on television, Gore, sullen, silent, and undeniably puffy, simply stared at

Franken, possibly in the knowledge that he was looking at the next president of the United States.

His recent successes have yet to go to Franken's head, perhaps because they never will. "I'm basically a very simple guy. I get up at four in the morning, I work hard, love my family, and I demand as much from others as I do from myself. And I've given up all my other projects to concentrate on one goal and one goal only: leading the world's only remaining superpower into the new millennium and beyond." ∎

10:45 P.M. TUCKING THE KIDS IN BY PHONE. "TELL MOMMY I LOVE HER AND MISS HER."

January 22, 2000

Spent day posing for ridiculous photos for Howard's big *Newsweek* story with me on treadmill, pretending to talk to kids on phone (actually dial tone), etc. Told him article better fucking be good.

January 23, 2000

Read Howard's cover story and told him I thought it was a little over the top. But Howard says that *Newsweek* readers are morons and the only people who are stupider are *Time* readers. Okay, he should know. Asked him if *Newsweek* will print article without checking out any of the things he made up. But he says he has threatened to quit if they change one word, laying groundwork for his upcoming resignation from periodical. Howard crafty. Not fully trustworthy. Must keep eye on him.

January 24, 2000

LATE CITY FINAL

Newsweek Scribe in Franken Fracas

Newsweek's longtime Washington bureau chief Howard Fineman abruptly quit the publication yesterday to sign aboard as press secretary for the skyrocketing campaign of *Saturday Night Live* alum Al Franken. Editors at the weekly were said to be furious with Fineman, whose glowing cover story on his new boss hits newsstands today. "I don't see how he could do this," said new managing editor Jonathan Alter. "He's compromised just about every standard of journalistic ethics I know."

"Jonathan Alter wouldn't know a journalistic ethic if it came up and chewed his pecker off," said a combative Fineman. "I quit, because, unlike Alter, whom I like personally, I refuse to be a toadying bootlicker." The timing of the article and the resignation raised eyebrows throughout the Fourth *(continued on next page) (continued from previous page)* Estate, though Fineman insists that it is a matter of pure coincidence. "Franken approached me and I accepted his offer after the article was put to bed. And I accepted the offer because I believe everything I wrote in that article to be true, namely that Al Franken should and will be elected the next leader of the world's only remaining superpower."

January 25, 2000

Frank Luntz and D on cloud nine about latest poll results, postdebate and post–*Newsweek* article. (Also post–*Post* item on Howard. Note to self: If Howard becomes campaign liability will need to cut him loose.) I lead Gore by 26 points. Good news for me, bad news for Gore!

January 26, 2000

Today's poll has me up by 32 points. Staff cannot agree on next step. N says despite huge lead I should not go on vacation. P suggests giant teach-in on structure of retail banking industry with Snoopy and blimp (how 'bout some new ideas, P?). Howard thinks fat lady's foot not sufficiently milked. Is he crazy? Hope I didn't make big mistake with Howard. D thinks time has come to approach Gore and offer him way out with honor. Dan likes sound of what D is saying. Luntz wants to conduct more research (big surprise). D and Dan have a majority. Asked Brenda? Brandy? to call to set up meeting.

January 27, 2000

N and Gore chief of staff haggling over details for summit meeting. I say Gore must come to me since I am front-runner. He says I must come to him since he is vice president. We agree to meet on neutral ground at Bob Kerrey headquarters.

January 28, 2000

Kerrey headquarters a dump! Gore not there when I arrived so I had to wait in coffee shop across street until he arrived so I could make him wait. He started in by saying that there was no excuse for my behavior during debate and if I had come to apologize, he would not accept it. I told him fat chance and that he should withdraw from race now to avoid embarrassing himself and wife Tipper further. He took offense about my mentioning wife, and I said, "Now you know how it feels." He said, "Now I know how *what* feels?" I said, "You know." And he said, "No, I don't." And I said, "My brother, you fool." And that made him mad all over again. I tried to calm him down and be statesmanlike by holding out possibility of his being my running mate. Said vice president is job he is clearly qualified for. Then he left, I guess to think it over.

Overall impressions of Gore: tall
puffy
thin-skinned
temperamental

January 29, 2000

Universal agreement that I will win Iowa caucuses tomorrow. Only size of margin in question. Now, on verge of victory, I am wondering if I really want to be president after all. I have seen more of America and Americans in past year than in entire previous lifetime and am not so sure I like what I see. If Iowa and New Hampshire are any indicator, country riddled with S.P. But without doubt, campaigning can be fun sometimes and have made lifelong friend in person of Dan Haggerty.

The Des Moines Register

DES MOINES, IOWA ■ TUESDAY, JANUARY 31, 2000 ■ PRICE 40 CENTS IN STORES/50 CENTS IN COIN RACKS

Franken Sweeps Iowa Caucuses By Largest Margin in History

■ Gephardt Weak Second; Wellstone Distant Third; Franken "Jubilant"

Gore Trails in Every Group Except Gay Males; Vows to "Fight On"

New Hampshire's Daily Newspaper

The Union Leader

Wednesday February 4, 2000

136th Year ©1998 Union Leader Corp., Manchester, NH "THERE IS NOTHING SO POWERFUL AS TRUTH" – DANIEL WEBSTER ★★★ 50¢ – Newsstand

FRANKEN TRIUMPHS IN DEMOCRATIC PRIMARY; REPUBLICANS GINGRICH, BUSH, BUCHANAN, FORBES, IN FOUR-WAY TIE

Gephardt, Kerrey, Bradley Withdraw from Race

Gore Distant Fifth, Vows to "Fight On"

Quayle Misses Primary Due to Scheduling Error

The Miami Herald

Final

www.herald.com

97th YEAR, No. 9
Copyright © 1996 The Miami Herald

WEDNESDAY, MARCH 11, 2000

35 Cents
For home delivery, call 305 350-2000

FRANKEN SWEEPS SUPER TUESDAY, BEATING GORE IN EVERY STATE, INCLUDING TENNESSEE

GOP VOTERS TURNED OFF BY BITTER BATTLE, RESULTING IN LOW TURNOUT AND FOUR-WAY TIE

Bush Call for "Healing" Angrily Rejected by Buchanan, Gingrich, and Forbes

ELECTION NEWS

■ **Democrats Mobilizing Behind Franken Juggernaut** *page 20*

■ **Quayle Withdraws After "Jose Jimenez" Gaffe** *page 21*

■ **Gore Vows to "Fight On"** *page 21*

Bank Teller New$

Vol. 3 Number 5 – March Issue   www.banktellernews.com

ASSOCIATION OF AMERICAN BANK TELLERS ENDORSES FRANKEN

Executive Committee Receptive to Anti-ATM Message

Los Angeles Times

CIRCULATION
1,395,150 DAILY / 1,600,386 SUNDAY

WEDNESDAY, JUNE 4, 2000
COPYRIGHT 2000 / THE TIMES MIRROR COMPANY/CC 132 PAGES

DAILY 75¢
DESIGNATED AREAS HIGHER

Franken Wins Primary, Clinching Nomination

GOP VOTERS FLOCK TO DEMOCRAT AFTER BUSH, FORBES, BUCHANAN, GINGRICH BROUHAHA

Quayle Offers Role as Peacemaker; Gore Vows to "Fight On" Despite Mathematical Elimination

---

The San Diego Union-Tribune

Friday
July 17, 2000

City Final
35¢

REPUBLICAN CONVENTION ENDS ABRUPTLY IN DISARRAY

Gingrich Cancels Acceptance Speech After Buchanan, Bush, and Forbes Threaten Disturbances; Quayle Offers Role as Mediator

Franken Describes Situation as "Sad"

Sunny
High 88, Low 56
Complete weather, 20C

THE DENVER POST

ON THE WEB
The Denver Post Online
www.denverpost.com

August 12, 2000

Voice of the Rocky Mountain Empire

★25¢ — May vary outside metro Denver

Franken Picks Lieberman as Running Mate

■ Connecticut Senator Describes Himself as "Pleased and Honored"; All-Jewish Ticket First Since Reconstruction

---

AL HAYAT

الحياة

طبعة نيويورك

٢٤ صفحة

للنشر بالعربية على الإنترنت

www.sakhr.com

إنّ الحياة عقيدة وجهاد

مفاوضات "واي" على حافة الانهيار بعد تهديد اسرائيل بالانسحاب

"الرئيس كلينتون خلال اجتماعه ليل الثلاثاء - الأربعاء، مع نتانياهو ومويديناي. (أ ب)"

□ واشنطن - رفيق خليل المعلوف

■ أفقدرت مفاوضات واي ريفر، في اليوم السابع من الانهيار...

التتمة في الصفحة (٦)

The Washington Post

FRIDAY, SEPTEMBER 9, 2000

BUCHANAN ANNOUNCES FORMATION OF ANTI-ABORTION, AMERICA-FIRST PARTY, FURTHER DIVIDING GOP FAITHFUL

Gingrich-Armey Trail Franken-Lieberman by 38 Percentage Points in Latest Poll

The New York Times

VOL. CXLVII   NEW YORK, TUESDAY, OCTOBER 2, 2000   60 CENTS

FRANKEN AND GINGRICH TEAMS FAIL TO AGREE ON FORMAT FOR DEBATES

Deputy Campaign Manager
Otto Franken Calls Gingrich–
League of Women Voters
Proposal "Looney Tunes"

THE NATION'S NEWSPAPER — OCT 30, 2000

USA TODAY

NO. 1 IN THE USA . . . FIRST IN DAILY READERS

Gingrich Negative Ads Backfire

Attack on Franken's brother is denounced by Candace Gingrich

THE WALL STREET JOURNAL

© 1999 Dow Jones & Company, Inc. All Rights Reserved.

VOL. CCXXXII NO. 52   EE/CP   NOVEMBER 4, 2000   INTERNET ADDRESS: http://wsj.com

Markets Up 437 Points In Anticipation Of Franken Victory

Broadbased Advance of More than 5.6 Percent Spurred by Leak of Steingarten Plan. Insurance Issues Set Pace. Bank Stocks Lag

NEW YORK POST

LATE CITY FINAL

WEDNESDAY, November 8, 2000   http://www.nypost.com/   . . . 50¢

PRINCE CHARLES KILLED IN POLO MISHAP!

PART THREE

THE
PRESIDENCY

THE VOID

THE FIRST ONE HUNDRED DAYS OF
THE FRANKEN PRESIDENCY

BOB WOODWARD

Introduction

WHEN AL FRANKEN was swept into office with the largest plurality in American electoral history, it was with the promise of filling the void between what Americans wanted from their leaders and what their leaders had been giving them. During the first hundred days, that void not only remained unfilled but was replaced by an even greater, more alarming void.

This is the story of that void.

Since most of the principals in the story I am about to tell remain in office, at least for the time being, the reader will appreciate that many of my sources did not wish to speak on the record for fear of retribution by President Franken or his brother Otto. In reporting any story as embarrassing as this one, it is important to state clearly the methodology governing the use of sources, who either insist on anonymity or on being referred to by someone else's name.

Many of the sources asked to be referred to as "Deep Throat," and I am sorry that I couldn't accommodate their wishes. The actual Deep Throat, Al Haig, was not a source.

Overall, more than 250 people were interviewed, some as many as 250 times, and a few by me personally. Only one person, Dick Morris, agreed to speak for attribution.

Dialogue and quotations have been recreated based on what I think the participants probably said. When someone is said to have "thought" or "felt" something, that description comes from my research assistant, Gary, who is particularly good at that kind of thing. When someone is said to have "smelt" something, Gary means that they either thought they smelt it or felt they smelt it. For all intents and purposes these concepts may be regarded as interchangeable.

Weather conditions cited were obtained from my editor's neighbor's son, Paul Zervos, a 33-year-old idiot savant, who can remember the weather conditions for every hour of every day of his life even though he is unable to dress himself without assistance.

Some of the sequences in the book are what I call "fantasy" sequences. These were episodes for which no sources were readily available or for which the primary source had died.

Copies of all documents, transcripts, and tape recordings, as well as Gary's notes and my hand-annotated copy of the first and only draft, have been deposited in a closet in my pool house, which I hope will establish once and for all that the cost of building, maintaining, and staffing my pool house is completely tax deductible. A duplicate set has been donated to the Woodward Library, which is being built underneath my tennis court. Both sets will be made available for study by scholars and the public in general in five hundred years. Once the archives are opened it will be clear that my methodology has been scrupulous and charges that my books are unduly speculative are baseless.

Some readers may quarrel that the choice of a hundred days is purely arbitrary and based solely on the fact that one hundred is a nice round number. These readers might argue, for example, that if I had chosen instead to write about the first one hundred and forty days or two hundred and twelve days or whatever, I might have been able to present a more complete picture of the crisis in leadership that gripped the Franken presidency from its very beginning. To them I can merely say that I have only been paid for a hundred days. So a hundred days it must be.

1

ALAN STUART FRANKEN took the oath of office as the nation's forty-fourth president just after twelve noon on a cold and windswept January 20th. An early morning rain shower had washed the Capitol steps clean of debris, but then turned to ice as a cold front swept across the District of Columbia. The temperature was a mere 22 degrees and falling, marking this as the coldest inauguration since the one during which William Henry Harrison contracted the pneumonia that would kill him just thirty-one days later.

President-elect Franken had set out from his temporary residence in Blair House with his family several hours before and made the one-and-seven-sixteenths-mile walk to the Capitol bareheaded, overcoatless, and trailed by a riderless horse, in one of the day's many Kennedy-esque overtones.

Now, as the barometric pressure dropped from 990 millibars to an ominously low 980 millibars, Franken arrived at the Capitol steps, ten minutes behind schedule, out of breath, and hoarse from shouting, "Hi, it's me!" to the crowd lining Pennsylvania Avenue. Thousands had been gathering since early that morning in hopes of catching a glimpse of the stocky Minnesota native who had stunned the nation less than three months earlier with his landslide victory over former House Speaker Newt Gingrich.

As he climbed the first of the Capitol's fifty-three steps, (one for each state, plus Guam, Puerto Rico, and the Philippines), Franken was greeted solemnly by Chief Justice William Rehnquist and Associate Justice Ruth Bader Ginsburg, upon whose family Talmud Franken would swear the oath of office.

After taking pains to see that his wife, Franni, and his children, Thomasin and Joe, were seated comfortably, and borrowing an overcoat from actor Dan Haggerty, Franken crossed the open space behind the podium to shake hands with and then hug his predecessor, William Jefferson Clinton, who remained seated and looked uncomfortable as Franken flung his arms around him.

Bill Clinton's chilly greeting of his heir was as chilly as the January air. Their relationship had been strained ever since Franken had declined to seek his advice after winning the party's nomination at the Denver convention six months prior. In explaining the lapse, Franken was rumored to have said, "Why do I need his advice? I already know how to get a blow job."

Noticeably absent was Vice President Albert Gore, Jr., who had broken with tradition and rebuffed the overtures of the Franken team. They had invited him to sit in a place of honor next to the President-elect's brother Otto, who had just been released from a North Korean prison.

Otto Franken had arrived on the dais at the last minute at the end of a remarkable journey, which had taken him from Seoul, South Korea, to the Demilitarized Zone to Pyongyang in the north and thence to Rhein-Main Air Base near Frankfurt, Germany, where he had been pronounced disease-free except for a flare-up of chlamydia. Military jets had been scrambled to get Otto to Washington just in time to see his brother inaugurated. The 52-year-old recovering alcoholic and sex addict looked tired and in need of a shave, but clearly happy as he placed his top hat and shopping bag on the empty seat to his left.

But as happy and as proud as Otto Franken was, he could be no happier or prouder than the six men who were seated in a group to the left (the audience's left) of the podium, the President-elect's senior staff and personal brain trust. They were:

- Norman J. Ornstein, the 51-year-old political scientist who had served Franken as campaign manager and had been rewarded with the powerful position of White House chief of staff.
- Peter Steingarten, 53, an economist and expert on special interest groups. It was Steingarten who had been responsible for the finances of the Franken campaign and who now, as secretary of the treasury–designate, would be responsible for the finances of the entire nation.
- Howard Fineman, 50, the journalist and TV talking head who would continue as Franken's press secretary.
- Dick Morris, 52, the once-disgraced campaign strategist who had made an astonishing comeback as Franken's media advisor and who over the next hundred days would organize and provide beepers for the White House staff.
- Joel Kleinbaum, 54, the chief campaign counsel and attorney general–designate, who was still suffering from parasites contracted during a vacation in Korea and shivered in the knife-edged breeze.
- Dan Haggerty, 57, the star of TV's *Grizzly Adams*, who had been the Franken campaign's Rosey Grier and had just been named as Franken's choice to be ambassador to the Court of St. James's in London.

These six men, who had come so far together, who now sat blinking in the cold January sunlight, had more in common than just their age and skin color. The entire *gestalt* of the *weltanschauung* of these former *wunderkinder* was characterized by a certain *gemütlich* attitude toward each other's *schadenfreude*.

At 11:00 A.M. precisely, the Marine band finished its performance of Franken's favorite song, Simon and Garfunkel's "Mrs. Robinson," with a clash of cymbals. Reverend Thaddeus Thorndike strode to the veneer-and-particleboard podium, his long white beard flapping in the seventeen-mile-an-hour breeze. The 61-year-old Presbyterian minister from Creamery, New Hampshire, bore an uncanny resemblance to an Old Testament prophet, a resemblance that was heightened by a pronounced preference for prayers and hymns of the "Terrible Swift Sword" variety. For today's invocation, Thorndike had chosen one of the grimmest and most terrifying passages from the entire Scripture, the chapters of Genesis in which God demands that Abraham make a human sacrifice of his son Isaac. In a short homily which followed, Reverend Thorndike reminded the crowd that God demands nothing more of us than our complete obedience to his will.

"Amen," said Peter Steingarten, who was standing to Morris's right.

When Dick Morris thought of obedience, he pictured loyal, dogged treasury secretary–designate Steingarten, Al Franken's personal Rumplestiltskin who had spun straw into gold in the early days of the campaign. After two decades at the American Enterprise Institute, Steingarten possessed one of Washington's most envied Rollodexes, brimming with names and private phone numbers of key players in the insurance and casino gambling industries. It was Steingarten whose fund-raising acumen had made possible the purchase of the massive amounts of television airtime so essential for Morris's wickedly effective ads.

After Reverend Thorndike had concluded his reading with an extended period of glaring, Nobel laureate Elie Wiesel read a lengthy passage from his Holocaust memoir, *Night*, about how prisoners were selected for certain work details. Morris, whose WASP-y movie star good looks had caused many to wonder whether he was or was not Jewish (he was), thought the choice of Wiesel was appropriate, but was concerned that, in the extreme cold, his message of the triumph of the human spirit in the face of overpowering evil might be lost on the shivering throng.

As Wiesel skipped to his next selection, a detailed description of daily life in the camps, Morris reflected on his own personal journey and the stunning comeback he had made from the dark days of 1996 when he had been ridiculed by late-night comedians as a toe-sucking pervert. While a lesser man might have disappeared into a twilight world of Internet sex and mail-order dominatrixes like Roger Stone had, the ruggedly handsome Morris considered his own temporary disgrace a wake-up call, and capped his pilgrimage through political purgatory with the stewardship of Franken's campaign. Though technically lower in rank and title than Ornstein, Fineman, Kleinbaum, and Steingarten, and equal to Haggerty, Morris was, in fact, Team Franken's heart and soul. Perhaps his greatest accomplishment had been the discovery and intellectual seduction of Elaine Kyriakis, an obese victim of the ATM crisis who ironically had lost her foot. Feet had caused Morris's downfall. A foot would be his salvation.

Looking past the thin and still somewhat emaciated concentration camp survivor, Morris glimpsed the familiar features of former house speaker Newt Gingrich, who had won only his home county of Cobb County, Georgia, along with isolated pockets of Idaho in the November general election. Morris knew every whisker, giant pore, and blotch of that face, better even, Morris thought, than Gingrich's second wife. Gingrich's familiar visage had been the unwitting superstar of a series of brilliant and decisive ads, which Morris had conceived and produced single-handedly, spending long nights in a darkened edit bay gradually "morphing" Gingrich's new, svelter self into his old bloated appearance. The image of Gingrich looking fat and sinister served as a shocking reminder of the ignominious days of the 1995 government shutdown and drove frightened voters by the millions into the Franken camp. "Hope," Morris liked to say, "is fleeting. But fear, fear is forever." Indeed, Morris felt a tinge of irrational fear as Gingrich's beady eyes momentarily locked with his.

But Morris knew he had no logical reason to be afraid of the now impotent and disgraced former speaker, who had become a national laughingstock, and flashed the Georgian one of Morris's hundred-Watt molar-baring smiles.

All things considered, this should have been Morris's finest hour.

But something was wrong.

Dick Morris was worried.

And he wasn't the only one. None of Franken's senior staff (except People's Choice Award–winner Haggerty, whom the President-elect had asked for some tips on performance) had seen the inaugural address that

Franken was about to deliver. Morris knew only that Franken had been working on it for days in isolation to prepare an address that he had told his confidants must be "both eloquent and memorable."

Shielded zealously by his loyal secretary and gatekeeper Brenda Jackson from all visitors except for his family, Franken had emerged only briefly, each time to request some seemingly unrelated piece of source material. One day it would be a copy of Kevin Costner's epic *Dances With Wolves*, the next, a videotape of *Nine to Five* starring Dolly Parton and Dabney Coleman.

Ornstein, bespectacled and wonkish, looked ill at ease in his ill-fitting morning suit, Morris thought, perhaps because even Norman Ornstein, godfather to the President-elect's son, who had been first to join the campaign and traveled the farthest with Al Franken, was completely in the dark.

Normally, Ornstein prided himself on his almost preternatural foreknowledge of what his boss was about to do or say. He liked to joke that he and Franken were "like Siamese twins joined at the brain." But this time, his eerie powers had failed him. Cornering Haggerty in a fit of desperation, Ornstein had pumped him for details, but the hirsute thespian would say only that the speech was a "winner" and one of the best he'd ever heard.

Ornstein thought, and Morris thought, that the speech had better be a winner. Al Franken had promised a lot of things to a lot of people in the past two years and now the time had come to begin getting out of having to deliver them.

2

AFTER WAVING TO A BABY seated on her mother's lap in the front row, the beaming Franken bounded to the podium and placed his hand on Justice Ginsburg's battered Torah. As the balding and near-sighted Chief Justice William Rehnquist administered the oath of office, Morris could not help but reflect on the irony of this moment. After all, Rehnquist had for years owned a home in a community governed by restrictive covenants that forbade the sale of real estate there to Jews. And yet here was Rehnquist swearing in the nation's first Jewish president. Ironic.

Franken swore the oath of office just as Morris had told him to, in a strong and clear voice, without a hint of sarcasm. The crowd fell silent as the shadow of the MetLife blimp passed over them, borne on the now nineteen-mile-an-hour breeze. With the words "so help me God," the Bill Clinton era came to an end just as it had begun: with unseasonably cool temperatures, even for January.

Franken, now finally president at last after waiting all morning, allowed a dramatic pause to heighten the theater of the moment. Then, as the Air Force's elite Blue Angels squadron screamed overhead, narrowly missing the MetLife blimp, Franken began to speak.

"President Clinton, Mrs. Rodham Clinton, Mr. Chief Justice, Mrs. Chief Justice, members of Congress, astronauts, ambassadors, my fellow Americans. Before I begin today's historic address marking the peaceful transition of power and celebrating the awe-inspiring majesty of our remarkable democratic process, the park service police have asked me to make the following announcement. They have found a six-year-old girl answering to the name of 'Molly,' who has become separated from her parents somewhere in the mall area.

"Molly's parents, if you can hear me, please identify yourselves to the nearest member of the park service police, who will escort you to the holding area."

Morris could barely conceal his surprise at this unexpected wrinkle. No president in recent memory had started an inaugural address this way. Morris couldn't help wondering if President Franken had made up the story of the little girl to begin the speech on a touchingly human note. "That's exactly what I would have done," thought Morris, "although I would have made the little girl slightly younger and possibly deaf."

Morris looked around to see how others were reacting to Franken's daring gambit. While most maintained a poker face, Haggerty clearly approved, offering a round of solitary applause, only to be shushed by Hillary Rodham Clinton as Franken continued.

"My fellow Americans, the Bible tells us in Ecclesiastes that there is both a time to kill and a time to heal. And while I am certain there will be a great deal of both during my administration, if you'll indulge me I would like to speak to you today about the latter of the two, healing.

"I see before me an America united, united in the knowledge that we are the world's only remaining superpower. And in the acceptance of all that that entails. But I also see before me a nation divided. Divided not only by the mighty Mississippi River or the majestic snowcapped peaks of the Rockies, but by class, by race, and, yes, by color.

"We are becoming two nations. One rich and white and Asian. The other poor and black and other. We must heal this rift to become one nation if we are to survive into the fourth millennium, barely one thousand years from today. Hence my subject, healing. I am not speaking of the false healing that comes from legislation or monetary outlay. I am talking of the true healing that comes from a sincere apology freely offered and gladly accepted. And so I am here today to offer an apology for what most agree is a black mark on America's history, the evil of slavery.

"Perhaps it is fitting that the first Jewish president should be the one to reach out his hand to the descendants of this horrible incident. I offer my hand not out of guilt, for I too am a son of the oppressed, as Elie Wiesel reminded us so eloquently during his reading, which was a little long, but very moving nonetheless. Indeed, when slavery was abolished in this country, my great-great-grandparents still lived as bonded serfs on a remote estate outside of what is now Krasnodar in the Russian Federation.

"But just as I offered forgiveness to the Russians, though heaven knows they have not asked for it, it is now time for me as both a Jew and a president, to ask the forgiveness of the great-great-grandsons and great-great-granddaughters of the American slaves.

"I am sorry.

"Let the word go forth, slavery was wrong.

"Two nights ago, as I was preparing this address, I happened to catch the movie *Mandingo* on Cinemax. And though the nudity and adult language make it inappropriate for younger viewers, I highly recommend this movie to anyone who wishes to understand this terrible time.

"Make no mistake, slavery was wrong!

"As the Mandingo buck, Mede, says in the movie after he has been brought to James Mason's plantation to be used as breeding stock, 'Massa, it beez wrong to sell a nigger like a plow horse.' He's right. It does beez wrong. It beez *very wrong*. Those words are as true today as when Ken Norton said them twenty-six short years ago. And I am here today to say that it was *wrong* to hunt escaped slaves down on horseback; it was *wrong* to boil slaves alive; and it was *wrong* to sell a black woman merely because her breasts had grown too droopy."

To Morris's perfectly attuned political instincts, the mere mention of boiling slaves was a grave error. Buttoning the top button on his cashmere Zegna overcoat against the now twenty-one-mile-an-hour breeze, Morris stole a quick glance at Ornstein, Fineman, Steingarten, and Kleinbaum to ascertain their reactions. The first three stared down at their shoes while Kleinbaum was shaking his head and attempting frantically to get President Franken's attention.

As Franken continued with apologies to Indians, Japanese Americans, and women, in each case drawing on a popular film for inspiration, Morris thought that Franken was leaving someone out. That there was someone to whom Franken would now owe a big apology. And that person was his chief spokesman, Howard Fineman.

3

AT PRECISELY 7:45 the following morning, as the temperature approached the day's high of 38 degrees, Howard Morton Fineman pulled up to the Northwest gate of the executive mansion in his anthracite black 1999 Jaguar Vanden Plus. The car, with its gray leather interior, moon roof, and CD changer, was Fineman's pride and joy. At age 50, Fineman had finally begun to enjoy the good things in life, after struggling for years to make ends meet on the meager salary of a journalist. It was his good fortune that on the very day he had left his job at *Newsweek* and joined up with the Franken campaign, Fineman's wife, Amy, had inherited a large sum of money from an uncle living in Hartford, Connecticut. The extra money had allowed Fineman to indulge his taste in fine motor cars, and it had paid for the imposing Norman chateau, which the Finemans had recently purchased in Wesley Heights from columnist Arianna Huffington and her ex-husband, oil heir Michael Huffington.

As Fineman continued up the drive toward the White House, he was already preparing himself for what he knew would be an uncomfortable first encounter with the White House press corps. The overnight coverage of President Franken's unorthodox inaugural address had been somewhat unreceptive and, in a few cases, downright hostile. Fineman had spent years on the receiving end of White House spin-doctoring. Now it was Howard Fineman's turn to do a little spin-doctoring of his own.

For the last several months Fineman had been fine-tuning his own skills in the art of political damage control by interpreting the comments of the irrepressible Franken, who liked to speak extemporaneously and off the cuff. At a fund-raiser in Napa Valley organized by insurers of wineries, for example, Franken had declared that he had found Caesar Chavez's toenail at the bottom of his glass of Pinot Noir and then mimed a spitting gesture into a nearby planter. The unenviable task of smoothing the ruffled feathers of the representatives from the crucial Hispanic, labor, and Hispanic labor voting blocs fell to Fineman, who succeeded by promising crucial concessions on the Beverly Hills leaf blower controversy, thereby assuring that the remark would go no further.

Fineman entered the White House press room shortly after eight. Sam Donaldson, seated in his usual seat in the first row immediately leapt to his feet, knocking over Fineman's assistant, Jerry Traub, who was passing out a heavily edited transcript of the previous day's address. This was not a good omen, Fineman thought. Jerry was not seriously hurt but Donaldson refused to apologize to him and even suggested that it was Traub's fault for being clumsy and in the way. "This is the big leagues, asswipe," Donaldson had said, drawing a laugh from most of his colleagues in the room. Fineman reflected that, if he were in their place, he might have laughed too. After all, Donaldson, though almost unimaginably cruel and self-centered, was funny, a gift Fineman envied him. He could use a good joke right now, Fineman told himself. Something to break the ice.

"Good morning, ladies and gentlemen," Fineman began with a straight face. "I just want to announce that as part of the Franken Administration's cost-conscious approach to government, from now on each of you will be limited to a single piece of danish before the morning briefing."

Donaldson was on his feet almost instantaneously. "What are you talking about? You don't give us any danish at all!"

"Uh-oh," Fineman thought, "I probably should have checked on that." From there the briefing would go from bad to worse. One exchange in particular would haunt Fineman for the remaining ninety-nine days of the first hundred days of the Franken Administration and probably long thereafter. Responding to a question from UPI's Helen Thomas about whether anyone had had anything positive to say about Franken's speech, the new press secretary quoted columnist Carl Rowan to the effect that the President's apology to African Americans had been "welcome," "eloquent," and "sincere."

Then, just as the relative humidity outside peaked at 42 percent, NBC's Claire Shipman, not generally regarded as one of the more combative members of the White House press corps, rose to take issue with Fineman's statement. Reading from Rowan's column, she pointed out that what he had *actually* written was that "Franken's apology would have been *welcome*, (italics mine) if it had been more eloquent and not so insincere."

Fineman responded by calling into question Shipman's patriotism, but it was too late. The damage had already been done.

4

"DON'T WORRY, HE'LL BE HERE," Norm Ornstein told the group assembled for the first formal meeting of Al Franken's Cabinet. The midwinter sun peeked out momentarily from the fluffy cumulus clouds that had obscured it on and off for most of the chilly afternoon, rendering the recessed halogen lighting installed during the energy-wasting Reagan era temporarily superfluous.

"Well, where the hell is he?" barked transportation secretary Arlen Specter. Convincing the Pennsylvania Republican to accept the transportation portfolio had been a feather in Ornstein's cap. But now, as minutes stretched into hours and the sun disappeared behind another cloud, rendering the halogen lighting useful again, the nervous chief of staff began to worry that Specter, and eventually the others, might get restless and leave.

Ornstein looked around at the thirteen handpicked Cabinet secretaries, every last one of them a son or daughter of Israel. The bold decision to name a Cabinet entirely composed of Jews had been Franken's and Franken's alone, made without hesitation the very night of his historic landslide victory. Ornstein, Fineman, Kleinbaum, and Morris, though Jewish themselves, had argued against the move, which Ornstein felt sent the "wrong message" to other traditionally Democratic constituencies such as blacks and Hispanics. Ornstein worried too that the press, mindful of the old canard about Jewish control of the news media, might be defensive and report the decision with something less than the blind, utter adulation that they had accorded Franken during his campaign. And in fact there had been some tentative criticism immediately after the all-Jew Cabinet was announced. The *Wall Street Journal*, in a signed editorial, had said that "while no student of history, financial or otherwise, would question the practical wisdom of a Cabinet made up entirely of Jews, any student of realpolitik must question its symbolic wisdom."

As so often happens, though, the public had other ideas. A *CBS News/New York Times* poll reported that an overwhelming percentage of the country agreed with President Franken's memorable logic, to wit that "the American people don't want a Cabinet that 'looks like America.' They want a Cabinet that the President is comfortable with."

But it did little good to the nation for the President to feel comfortable with his Cabinet if, in fact, he was not actually *with* them as indeed now he was not, thought Ornstein. Their limited store of small talk exhausted, the silence in the Cabinet Room grew deafening with the ticktock of the large presentation clock on the wall setting everyone's nerves on edge. After his stomach growled audibly, newly minted Treasury Secretary Steingarten tried to lighten the moment by commenting that "you get thirteen Jews in a room, you'd think at least there'd be something to eat."

"Fourteen! Fourteen Jews!" vice-president Joe Lieberman reminded the Treasury Secretary, drawing a laugh from most of the Cabinet and a sigh of relief from Ornstein. "Thank God for Joe," Ornstein whispered to himself, remembering the lucky inspiration that had led Franken to offer the centrist Connecticut senator the second spot on the ticket. At the time, Franken had argued for his choice by saying that Lieberman would "balance the ticket since he's Orthodox and I'm Reform." Lieberman, however, had needed some convincing. When Dick Morris had first brought him the offer, Lieberman was incredulous and said that "Franken will get us both killed." But it was ultimately Ornstein's insistence that it would be a "schande for the goyim" if Lieberman refused, which had won the senator over. And at this very moment, Norman Ornstein was very, very thankful that the universally respected and even-keeled legislator had finally said yes.

Ornstein's reverie was interrupted by Treasury Secretary Steingarten, who was putting his potent organizational skills to good use by organizing lunch. "Okay, I can't read this. Who has . . . it looks like "Moo Shu Duck?" The yellow legal pad had only gone halfway around the table and already there was confusion about the order. "And they haven't even begun discussing which restaurant to order from," Ornstein thought. He knew that some would insist on Empire Garden, which had good food, while others would argue for the Szechuan Palace, which was closer. This was turning into a nightmare.

"That's me. I have the Moo Shu," said Harold Lipsky, the former CEO of the giant Metropolitan Life insurance company, who had been appointed to head the Department of Health and Human Services.

"Hey, we haven't decided where we're going to order from yet. My order depends on where we order from," said Leonard Shapiro, Lipsky's former deputy at MetLife, who was now secretary of commerce.

"All I care about is which place has better Orange Chicken," said secretary of the interior Ralph Lauren (né Lipschitz). "That's all that matters to me."

"Well, fine, if that's how we're going to decide, based on the Orange Chicken, then it's definitely the Empire Garden. There is no question that they have the best Orange Chicken in town." It was Morris, decisive and well informed as always.

"That's crap! If we order from there it'll take nine hours!" said Madeleine Albright, one of three holdovers from the Clinton Administration.

"Yeah, I'm hungry," said Secretary of Agriculture Dan Glickman, also a Clinton veteran. "Orange Chicken that's here in twenty minutes is a lot better than Orange Chicken that's here in two hours. Boy, you'd think thirteen starving Jews would at least be able to agree on that, right, Bill?"

Defense Secretary William Cohen, the third returning Cabinet member, responded with just the barest hint of irritation. "Dan, I've told you before, I'm not Jewish!"

This drew a laugh from the entire group except Albright.

"Sure you're not, Bill," Sandy Koufax, the Dodger great, now secretary of veterans affairs, joked. "Only your parents were Jewish."

Cohen looked upward in exasperation and grunted while Albright scowled. Outside it began to be slightly more sunny.

"I'm not afraid to admit I'm Jewish," shouted Harvey Golub, the new secretary of housing and urban development, whose years of stewardship of American Express as its CEO had impressed President-elect Franken, a card member since 1967. "And I want sesame noodles."

In the laughter and good-natured shouting that followed, Ornstein slipped away to search for the missing President.

Climbing the stairs to the third-floor private residence in the West

Wing of the White House, Ornstein passed servants, aides, and secretaries scurrying to and fro, either hard at work or doing a damn good job of faking it. He could, of course, stop any one of them—or any one of the innumerable Secret Service agents for that matter—and ask them if they had seen the President and, if so, which way he had gone. Ornstein resisted the urge to do so, however, fearing that it might seem odd that the chief of staff did not know where the President was.

As chief of staff, Ornstein was the only person, besides members of the President's immediate family, Dan Haggerty, and Sandy Koufax, with permission to enter the private areas of the White House at any time. "The President's in there, isn't he?" Ornstein asked Brock McCafferty, a Secret Service agent assigned to the President's personal security detail who happened to be stationed outside the door to the President's bedroom.

"Yes, sir," McCafferty answered. "He is."

"And, uh, he hasn't left there in four days, has he?"

"No, sir, he hasn't."

If McCafferty found this at all strange, his impassive expression did not betray it. He stood silently as Ornstein hovered indecisively just outside the door, afraid of what he might find if he carried out his mission and entered the bedroom.

"Let me ask you something, Agent . . . ?"

"McCafferty."

"Let me ask you something, Agent McCafferty. Have you noticed anything strange about the President's behavior?"

"Well, it isn't really my place to say, sir, but, compared to other presidents I've served, President Franken seems to be watching an awful lot of television."

Ornstein steeled himself for the worst and pushed open the door.

As soon as he entered, Ornstein tripped over a tightly stretched vacuum cleaner cord. Franni Franken was busily pushing a large upright Hoover around the green carpet of the room. Al Franken, wearing pajamas, was lying in bed, bathed in the blue light of a large television set. Newspapers and magazines were scattered around the room and Ornstein noted with some concern that most were opened to stories on the Inaugural, particularly stories on the President's speech. Al Franken looked like he was lying at ground zero of the hundred-megaton explosion of hostile coverage that had greeted his by-now infamous address.

"The Honeymoon Beez Over!"

"A Sorry Excuse for an Apology"

"Apologize for Dat Speech, Massa!"

"Ken Norton Says Speech 'Constructive,' 'Helpful.' "

"Rowan Calls Fineman 'Liar' and 'Scumbag.' "

The headlines told the whole story. The Inaugural Address of President Al Franken had gotten his administration off on the wrongest of wrong feet in American history. Franken, who could do nothing wrong during his miraculous campaign, had stepped in an enormous bucket, chock-full of America's most foul waste product: racial insensitivity.

Stepping over copies of *Time* and *Newsweek*, which had for the first time in their history both run the same cover line—"It Beez a Massive Error in Judgment"—Ornstein approached the near-catatonic chief executive.

"Mr. President? Sir?"

Al Franken did not respond, but Franni Franken, seeing Ornstein for the first time, turned off the vacuum cleaner.

"Hi, Norm. Can you believe this?"

She gestured toward the President.

"Go on! Get up! Get dressed! What the hell's the matter with you?!" Mrs. Franken shouted in her husband's ear, while sixty-thousand feet above her a dark cumulonimbus thunderstorm cloud formed with a heavy base and anvil-shaped top.

But the President just covered his head with a pillow. "It was like this after his Stuart Smalley movie bombed," the First Lady offered, shaking her head resignedly.

"But he's the President now!" Ornstein said, with a tinge of hysteria beginning to show through his normally unflappable demeanor. "He's the President! He can't do this!" the chief of staff gasped as he struggled unsuccessfully to wrestle away the pillow that was covering the chief executive's face.

"Shouting at him's no good, Norm," Franni Franken said, laying a hand on Ornstein's arm, "Believe me, I've tried. And he's not going to let go of that pillow either. Not till he's done sulking."

"Well, how long will that take?"

At that very moment Franni Franken didn't know how long it would take. She knew only that if her husband's disturbing behavior continued much longer, she would return with the children to the Franken's comfortably appointed seven-room apartment on Manhattan's Upper West Side. But for now, she had vacuuming to do.

Returning to the first floor of the East Wing, past stacks of unpacked boxes that still lined the hallway almost a full week after the inauguration, Ornstein battled desperately to control his own mounting panic. He would have to put the best face on the situation for the Cabinet. But how?

When Ornstein reentered, the yellow legal pad was making its third circuit of the Roosevelt Room as the Cabinet put the finishing touches on its order of Chinese food. "Norm, I ordered steamed dumplings for you," said Peter Steingarten, oblivious to any hint of discomposure on his old friend's face. "I know that's what you usually get."

"Steamed dumplings will be fine, Peter. Thank you. But before we phone in the order, I should tell you that I don't think we're going to be having this meeting today after all."

A collective groan escaped from the Cabinet. Ornstein gestured for quiet, preemptively eliminating the opportunity for any sarcastic remarks. "The President is a bit under the weather," he said. "He may have picked up that bug that's been going around, from standing out there in the cold during Elie Wiesel's reading. But he told me to tell you that he appreciates your being here today and looks forward to hammering out a vigorous agenda with you when we hit the ground running tomorrow. So same time here tomorrow."

"Why doesn't Joe just do it?" Dan Glickman suggested. "Since we're all here and we've got food coming."

Lieberman rose from his chair. "While I appreciate your confidence in me, Dan, the American people elected Al Franken to be not only *their* leader but ours, as well."

"Hear, hear," said diminutive Interior Secretary Lauren as the others nodded in solemn approval.

"Okay, so what are we going to do about the food?" Harvey Golub wanted to know.

"I'm calling it in now," said Commerce Secretary Shapiro, with a phone held to his ear, "So, if we're *not* going to eat, someone better tell me."

"I know the President would want you to enjoy your Chinese food and use this as an opportunity to get to know each other informally and perhaps discuss, informally also, of course, the fastest and most politically efficient way to dismantle the remaining provisions of the Glass-Steagle Act," Ornstein said.

As Shapiro gave his Visa number to Boy-wah Ling, 31, a recent immigrant from the Shandung Province in China who considered himself very lucky to have found work as a waiter at the Szechuan Palace restaurant despite his limited command of English, Norm Ornstein reflected that the Cabinet would not be so easily mollified next time by mere Chinese food. President Franken would *have* to attend tomorrow's meeting in person. Or there would be trouble. Serious trouble.

5

BUT PRESIDENT FRANKEN did not attend the next day's Cabinet meeting. Nor the one the day after that. Nor any other meeting for that matter. In fact, as midwinter turned to late-midwinter, President Franken did not leave his bedroom or, indeed, his bed for the next three weeks. His inner circle, increasingly desperate, employed every conceivable excuse to explain the President's absence from the public eye.

Perhaps the most difficult task during this most difficult time fell to Howard Fineman, who faced an increasingly restive and impertinent press corps each morning at his daily briefing. Having no presidential schedule to go over and no events from the previous day to report on only left more time open for questions, embarrassing questions. Fineman was obliged to fall back on a standard defense that he would be "happy to answer questions about the President's whereabouts and activities at such time as that becomes appropriate" over and over again.

Finally, even ambassador-designate Dan Haggerty, who had heretofore been immune to the general sense of despair and panic, agreed that the time had come for drastic measures. On a partly cloudy Tuesday afternoon, Haggerty had gone to the residence with Ornstein to try one last time to remove the pillow from President Franken's face. Haggerty succeeded only in tearing the pillow apart and covering the President with feathers and bits of Dacron™ foam, the pillow being of the "composite" variety that is filled with both materials.

It was Treasury Secretary Steingarten who volunteered for the task of locating a suitable physician to treat the sense of malaise that now hung over the President. It was decided that an ideal candidate would be the highest ranking Jewish doctor in the military, who could be counted on to appreciate the delicate nature of the President's condition.

Rear Admiral Lawrence Itzkowitz, M.D., adjutant-in-charge of the Navy's Psychiatric Command, was spirited secretly into the East Wing of the Executive Mansion on an unseasonably warm February evening. Puddles of melted snow had muddied Admiral Itzkowitz's standard issue black lace-ups, and he paused before entering the President's residence to wipe his feet.

At age 63, Itzkowitz was long past the peak of his military career. But by the sound of Ornstein's voice when he had summoned Itzkowitz to the White House, the admiral knew that the task before him would require every ounce of medical know-how and military discipline at his disposal. And as the admiral stepped into the President's bedroom and surveyed the scene before him, he regretted having told his wife everything that Ornstein had said over the phone. His wife, Sylvia, had a big mouth, Dr. Itzkowitz thought, that was her one failing.

President Franken, surrounded by his inner circle of aides and advisors, was sitting up in bed watching television. That's a good sign, thought Itzkowitz. He's sitting up. After saluting smartly, he began a cursory examination of the chief executive. "Mr. President," he asked, "have you been having any trouble sleeping?" The President did not respond except to gesture impatiently that Dr. Itzkowitz was blocking his view of *Caroline in the City*, starring spunky actress Lea Thompson, whom Itzkowitz recognized immediately from her gratuitous nude scene opposite Tom Cruise in the movie *All the Right Moves*.

The admiral withdrew to a nearby sitting room with Ornstein, Steingarten, Fineman, Kleinbaum, and Morris. It was the attorney general who spoke first. "He's crazy, right?" Kleinbaum said. "He's completely lost it, hasn't he?"

Itzkowitz was noncommittal. "I'll need to draw some blood before I make any sort of definitive diagnosis. But by the look of it, I'd say he's suffering from extreme depression. Has anything happened in the past month that could have set this off?"

The Inner Circle traded glances for a long minute before Itzkowitz broke the ice and said, "I'm kidding, of course. I was at the Inauguration and . . . oy!"

Fineman spoke. "Doctor, I'm sure you understand the need for absolute secrecy on this. We simply can't tell the American people that their president is suffering from an incapacitating emotional disability. I don't need to tell you that there is still a stigma attached to mental illness, particularly for someone in a position of great responsibility, like the President is."

"Epstein-Barr," Dr. Itzkowitz said quietly.

"What? What's that?" Ornstein asked.

"Epstein-Barr."

6

HOWARD FINEMAN entered the White House briefing room with a spring in his step. For the first time in weeks, he actually had something to say.

"Ladies and gentlemen, I have a brief statement I'd like to read, and then I'd be happy to answer your questions."

"Yeah, right," Sam Donaldson shouted sarcastically.

Fineman ignored the toupeed blowhard and continued. "The President's physician, Rear Admiral Lawrence Itzkowitz, has determined, after an exhaustive battery of tests, that the President is suffering from chronic fatigue syndrome, a disease which is caused by the Epstein-Barr virus. That's Epstein, E-p-s-t-e-i-n, Barr, B-a-r-r. Dr. Itzkovitz is treating the President here in the White House and is expecting the President to make a full and complete recovery. Furthermore, the admiral does not anticipate any need for the President to be hospitalized or institutionalized and believes that the President can continue to carry out his duties unimpeded by this one hundred percent–curable ailment."

The senior member of the White House press corps, UPI's Helen Thomas, shot up from her chair, dislocating her hip in the process. "Isn't chronic fatigue syndrome just a euphemism for depression?" she asked, gritting her teeth against the scaring pain of this, her third hip dislocation in as many days.

"Most definitely not, Helen. I think if you ask anyone who suffers from chronic fatigue syndrome, they'll tell you it's a very real disease that's physical in nature. Sometimes the disease *can* be accompanied by a certain understandable downturn in the patient's mood and general outlook, though this is not the case with respect to the President, who remains upbeat, though somewhat lethargic."

"Why hasn't the President been seen in public since the inauguration?" Sam Donaldson demanded to know. "Is this disease contagious? Some of us have families. I think we should be told."

"Sam, let me assure you that no one in this room is in any immediate danger of catching any sort of disease from the President. This isn't the Kennedy Administration, after all," Fineman joked. "But Dr. Itzkowitz does believe that for the time being it's best that the President remain isolated from any contacts that are not absolutely necessary."

"So he is contagious!" Sam bellowed. "I'm getting out of here!"

With Donaldson leading the charge, the press corps rushed out of the Briefing Room and out onto the South Lawn, still damp as result of an unusually low dew point, a phenomenon too complicated to go into here.

Press Secretary Fineman was left standing at the podium alone. And, for the first time in weeks, Howard Fineman was smiling.

7

IN THE FOUR WEEKS that followed, President Franken's constantly improving mood brought new light and new life to his administration. As the sophisticated "cocktail" of serotonin-selective reuptake inhibitors (SSRIs) took hold of Franken's psyche, the President's bedroom become a whirlwind of activity. Aides came and went, bills were drafted and redrafted, meetings were held, all so that the last vestiges of the Glass-Steagle Act be eradicated once and for all, freeing large insurance companies to enter the retail banking sector where Franken had always believed they belonged.

And so it came to pass that on a brisk, sun-drenched first day of spring, during which blustery seventeen-mile-an-hour winds from the northwest blew high cirrostratus clouds across the upper atmosphere, President Franken marched jauntily into the Rose Garden to sign the legislative cornerstone of his campaign agenda. Like the President himself, The Banking Competition and Native American Gaming Bill of 2001 had been bruised and bloodied but never defeated during its journey through the legislative process. Several unavoidable pork-barrel provisions had been added, including funding for a monorail linking several obsolete military bases in West Virginia. It had been a small price to pay to get Senator Byrd to shut up and invoke cloture.

Dick Morris and the rest of the President's advisors smiled broadly as Franken tossed handfuls of ceremonial pens into the air and hugged Admiral Itzkowitz impulsively.

They had much to smile about.

The Franken Administration had weathered a crisis of potentially devastating proportions. But now, as the Dow burst into record territory above the 14,000 level, Bill Gates's wealth topped 100 billion dollars, and the President's popularity was on the upswing, the disaster of the inaugural address appeared to be fading from the public's memory. Even Sam Donaldson, who had finally given up wearing his protective surgical mask during encounters with the President, shot Fineman a thumbs-up. Fineman thought that, by dropping the mask, Donaldson was sending *ABC News* viewers a valuable message: that the President was no longer diseased.

"You can't buy the kind of good publicity that you get when a guy like Sam Donaldson stops wearing a surgical mask around you," Fineman whispered to Steingarten. Steingarten wasn't so sure that there was *any* kind of publicity you couldn't buy, but smiled and nodded to Fineman nonetheless.

And indeed Al Franken appeared to have had his normally exuberant high spirits miraculously restored. Pointing to members of the crowd, kissing women in the front row of seats, and shadowboxing playfully with Jim Sits-by-the-fire, the honorary chief of the Davenport, Iowa, branch of the Ogalala Sioux, Franken worked the crowd like the man who had electrified the electorate only five months before.

As the wind dropped another mile and a half per hour, Franken strode confidently to the podium, picked up the remarks carefully crafted for him by Ornstein, Steingarten, and Morris, and began to read in a strong, clear voice. With the crowd cheering Franken's time-tested message of free markets and lower ATM fees, to Ornstein it almost seemed that the clock had been turned back to the heady days when candidate Franken could do no wrong. There was no doubt about it, the first two months of the Franken Administration had taken years off all of their lives and Ornstein doubted that any of them would ever make as complete a re-covery as the President appeared to have.

Concluding his prepared remarks with a call for the eventual total abolition of ATM fees, Franken announced that he had a personal statement to make. Norm Ornstein held his breath. This was where Al Franken had gotten into trouble last time.

"Some of you may have heard that I've been a little down lately. In fact, I want to read to you a letter I got from a little girl, Daisy Bertram of Independence, Missouri . . ."

There was no letter, Ornstein knew. The President had not been per-mitted to receive any sort of communication from the outside world ever since the media accounts of the inaugural address sent him into a tailspin.

"Daisy wrote, 'Dear Mr. President, my teacher, Mrs. Cadwaller, says that you aren't feeling well. I hope you get better soon. Love, Daisy.' Daisy, I want you to know that letters like yours made all the difference to me dur-ing my recent incapacitation and that, thanks to your prayers and good wishes, and the prayers and good wishes of millions of people like you across this great land, I am feeling better and better every day. Thank you, Daisy."

"Phew," thought Ornstein, "that was close."

"Oh, and one more thing," President Franken added, as Ornstein gripped Steingarten's upper arm in abject terror. "I'm feeling so good about myself, my team, and the direction this country is going, that I've decided to have myself cloned. Thank you."

"Hold on, Mr. President," Sam Donaldson yelled as he put his mask back on. "Did I hear you right? You're having yourself cleaned?"

"No, Sam. *Cloned*. Contrary to what you may have heard, I'm per-fectly capable of cleaning myself. Now, if you'll all excuse me, I have an appointment at the National Institutes of Health."

As President Franken exited to strains of "Hail to the Chief," Ornstein turned to his left and looked at the empty chair where just an instant before Press Secretary Fineman had been sitting.

Ornstein thought he caught a glimpse of Fineman running full-out across the South Lawn as if being chased by a swarm of bees. But Ornstein knew it was not imaginary insects that Fineman was running from, it was the grim reality that the President of the United States was about to submit himself to an unproven and highly controversial experimental scientific procedure.

8

THE CELLS from the inside of President Franken's cheek were busily dividing in a nutrient broth at the National Institutes of Health, oblivious to the storm that raged outside. The barometric pressure had been dropping steadily since midmorning and now rain and wind lashed the Washington, D.C., area. But there was another sort of storm that raged around the President's cheek cells. It was a storm of controversy.

Controversy over the cheek cells and the decision that had brought them to the nutrient broth in Bethesda.

Gary Bauer of the Family Research Center, a leading spokesman for the right-to-life movement, called the President's attempt to clone himself "an unconscionable attempt to play God"; The New Yorker's Joe Klein, who had stuck by Franken through thick and thin, described the cloning as "politically tone-deaf and an act of supreme egotism"; Elie Wiesel told Charlie Rose that President Franken's cloning attempt "carried echoes of the worst excesses of Dr. Mengele and the Nazi perversion of science." On the other hand, The American Cloning Society, Scientists for Cloning, and former president Gerald Ford all expressed varying degrees of support.

Fourteen miles to the southeast of the rapidly dividing cells, the President's inner circle was gathered in one of the most hastily convened of the many hastily convened meetings they had attended during the short time that Al Franken had been in office. So hastily, in fact, had this meeting been convened, that Ambassador-designate Dan Haggerty was not in attendance, but instead sleeping off a bender underneath a workman's tarpaulin in one of the rooms on the third floor of the White House that was currently undergoing renovation.

"You guys are supposed to be protecting my brother!" Otto Franken yelled.

"How can we protect him if he's going to go and do something crazy like clone himself?" Fineman protested.

"Now, did you just hear yourself?" the President's brother said menacingly. "You just said something very interesting. You just called my brother 'crazy.' "

"No, Otto," Fineman said, trying to control his temper, "what I said was that announcing to the American public that your first decisive action as president is to have yourself cloned is a crazy thing to do."

"That's *your* job!" Otto yelled, confusing everybody.

"*What* exactly is my job, Otto?" Fineman commented acidly. "Cloning your brother? That seems to be the job of the National Institutes of Health."

"Now, now, everybody," Ornstein interrupted as Otto reached for a nearby board. "Let's just take a deep breath and count to ten. Otto, there's beer in the pantry down the hall. Just help yourself."

It had been Morris's idea to spread beer throughout the White House as a way of controlling the volatile Otto Franken, who had been appointed Drug Czar over the objections of many.

With the President's brother safely sealed in the pantry thanks to a "malfunctioning" doorknob, the Inner Circle could get down to business.

"What the fuck are we going to do about this fucking guy?" said Sandy Koufax.

"The President or his brother?" Treasury Secretary Steingarten asked.

"Both of them! Correct me if I'm wrong, but doesn't cloning have something to do with reproducing genes? Why the fuck would we want to reproduce those genes?"

"Now, Sandy," Ornstein reminded the former Dodger southpaw, "we are talking about the President of the United States."

"Yeah, yeah. And the leader of the world's only remaining super-power," Koufax said, making a jack-off gesture with his celebrated pitching hand.

"That's a little disloyal," said Dick Morris, a man who counted loyalty as one of his own many virtues. "If it wasn't for Al Franken, Sandy Koufax wouldn't be secretary of veterans affairs."

"Right. And on behalf of twenty-six million loyal veterans, let me just say the man is not the most egg-shaped egg in the egg carton."

In the uncomfortable silence that followed, broken only by a clap of thunder from a ten-thousand-amp discharge of lightning, Admiral Itzkowitz stunned the room by saying quietly, "This is all my fault." Dick Morris had to admire the avuncular naval psychiatrist. Admitting one's mistake displayed the sort of personal courage that, of the Inner Circle, only Morris truly understood.

"When I first began treating President Franken, I was operating under certain diagnostic and psychopharmacological assumptions. That the President was suffering from depression was clear. What I did not know then was that this depression was symptomatic of an underlying bipolar disorder. And by merely treating the depression, I'm afraid I may have exacerbated its polar opposite condition, which is characterized by the sort of manic grandiosity that might inspire a man with the power to do so to have himself cloned."

"Well, can you fix him?" Steingarten asked.

"Peter, the good news is that manic depression, like the depression that I originally thought the President was suffering from, is highly treatable. The depression component responds well to one of the SSRIs, the manic phase we treat with lithium, and for the collateral loss of attention span and lethargy we usually prescribe Ritalin.

"The bad news is that it may take a while before we can determine the precise mix of drugs to give the President to deal with his particular condition. In the meantime, while we tinker with the dosage, you can expect more erratic behavior."

"Perhaps," Norm Ornstein thought, "it would have been a good idea to have gotten a second opinion from someone outside the somewhat less competitive military medical establishment at the outset." But Ornstein knew that it was too late for that. "Very well, Doctor," he said aloud, "proceed."

"Yes, sir. Where is the President now? I want to get these new drugs into his system as soon as possible," the admiral said.

"The last time I saw him, he was in the Oval Office calling old college friends," Steingarten reported.

"That's very manic. Let's go."

Ornstein and Itzkowitz headed out in search of the President. "As soon as this is all over, I'm going to take care of these boxes," the chief of staff promised himself.

9

NELSON ROLIHLAHLA MANDELA, the first black presi-
dent of South Africa, had been waiting with fifty members of the international press all afternoon to see the President of the United States. As the
clock on the mantel chimed the passage of another hour, Mandela got up
and began absently prodding the fire that was burning in the nearby fireplace
despite the near-60-degree (58.7 degrees, to be exact) April weather outside.

The Nobel Peace Prize–winner knew little about President Franken
except that he was said to be opposed to ATM fees. Mandela, who had
spent his life fighting the morally repugnant system of apartheid, thought
ATM fees were a peculiarly minor issue to be so passionate about.

Giving a burning log a vigorous poke with the antique wrought-iron
fireplace poker that, legend had it, Dolly Madison had rescued from the
burning White House in 1814, Mandela wondered where Franken could
be and whether the rumors that the President had been suffering from
paranoid delusions recently could possibly be true.

When the President entered the Rose Room, shutters clicked and
motor drives whirred. Mandela turned to greet Franken with the poker
still in hand. The 83-year-old African leader would later joke that it probably would have been better if Dolly Madison had never rescued that fireplace poker, because then Al Franken would never have mistaken it for a
weapon and never would have punched him in the stomach.

10

TWENTY MINUTES LATER in Norm Ornstein's office, the President's advisors passed around black-and-white enlargements of photographs taken earlier in the Rose Room.

"How do you want to spin this, Howard?" Ornstein inquired.

"Could we say that Mandela tripped and the President caught him with his fist?"

"No, Peter," Fineman replied. "It's on videotape."

Dick Morris, as usual, had a refreshingly original take on the unfortunate incident. "Is there any possibility that Mandela actually was attacking the President with the poker or that we could say he was? He did have kind of a crazy look in his eye."

"That was only *after* the President punched him in the stomach," Ornstein answered. "And besides, Dick, Nelson Mandela is the most universally revered leader in the world today. No one is going to believe that he attacked the President with a fireplace poker."

"In fact," Attorney General Kleinbaum said, "we have more the opposite problem. There's a very real danger that the President could be charged with assault and taken into custody by federal marshals. The evidence is right there on CNN."

"Oh, for Christ's sake, Joel," Drug Czar Otto Franken chimed in, pouring a Michelob on the attorney general's head, "you are more useless than tits on a bull."

Passing Kleinbaum a hand towel, Ornstein responded decisively to the threat of the President's imminent arrest. "Joel, get your people to draft a statement for Mandela to sign declining to press charges. Tell them there's an extra hundred million in foreign aid if he agrees to play ball."

"Aren't we all beating around the bush here?" Fineman asked pointedly. "We all know what the problem is."

"You're right," said Ornstein. "And where is Admiral Itzkowitz anyway?"

11

"NORM, I DON'T KNOW WHY you're so opposed to my going to Baghdad and killing Saddam Hussein personally," President Franken said as he took another Zoloft.

Ornstein was beginning to wonder whether all these pills were doing the President more harm than good. Sometimes the chief of staff even longed for the time not so long ago when the President spent the entire day in bed watching television. At least that was better than dealing with a new and ever more bizarre plan every fifteen minutes.

He had been unable to stop the cloning. The President's genetic twin was now gestating in the womb of lesbian actress Anne Heche. But he had been able to head off the proposed severing of diplomatic relations with Great Britain after the British government declined to receive the credentials of Ambassador Dan Haggerty. He had also been able to talk Franken out of taking Spanish lessons for three hours every day, arguing that it was not a good use of the nation's time.

But this latest scheme, the assassination of a foreign leader carried out personally by a sitting American President, had driven Ornstein to the brink of despair. What worried him even more was that Franken had informed him of the plan relatively late in the game, suggesting that others, including almost definitely the President's brother Otto, had enabled the President's latest flight of fancy.

"Mr. President, who besides your brother Otto is involved in this?"

"What makes you think Otto has anything to do with it?"

"Well, for starters, the plan calls for you to hit Saddam Hussein on the head with a board."

"It's not a board. It's a ceremonial plaque. He'll think it's a gift."

"Mr. President, how do you plan to escape?"

"Norm, have you read the latest CIA analysis on the situation over there?"

"I confess I haven't, sir."

"Well, you should. It's how Otto got the idea in the first place. The CIA says that the Republican Guard surrounding Saddam actually hates him and is looking for any excuse to drive him from power. My hitting him with the board, excuse me, the *plaque*, will be the spark that ignites a democratic revolution in Iraq. Norm, I don't want to go down in history as the president who ruptured Nelson Mandela's spleen. This is my bid for redemption."

"Sir, we're only eighty-five days into your presidency. You have four years, and very likely eight, to leave your legacy."

"Believe me, Norm, I know that. Killing Saddam Hussein is just the beginning."

Back in his office Norman Ornstein struggled to get a grip on himself. He wished there was some other way, but he knew what he had to do. After adjusting the thermostat in response to a sudden rise in the outside air temperature, Ornstein picked up his phone and rang Howard Fineman on a secure line. "Howard, what magazine do you want to work for when you leave the administration?"

12

THE APRIL 18TH ISSUE of *Time* magazine featured a cover with a photograph of an aggressive-looking Al Franken superimposed over a map of Iraq. "Exclusive!" the cover line blared. "Inside the Administration's Secret Plan to Kill Saddam."

Illustrated with an artist's conception of the proposed April 20th "boarding" of Hussein, the cover story detailed the entire plot. President Franken, wearing camouflage and holding the richly engraved plaque in his lap, was already airborne when word of the article reached *Air Force One*.

Franken was unfazed and wanted to proceed to Baghdad, though he admitted that the article might compromise the element of surprise. "We'll just go to Plan B," the chief executive said decisively.

"Plan B? And what would that be, sir?" either Ornstein or Fineman asked, Morris would recall later.

"Instead of hitting Saddam with the plaque, I'll strangle him. See, he'll be watching for the board, I mean plaque. This article may be a blessing in disguise."

"Right on, Al!" Otto Franken slurred, while stumbling "accidently" into Polly Cross, a 22-year-old Naval attaché, who served as a flight attendant aboard *Air Force One*. After steadying himself by grabbing Cross's breasts, the President's brother high-fived a bewildered Peter Steingarten, who had argued that his own presence aboard *Air Force One* was superfluous to the mission of murdering Saddam Hussein. The President had overruled him though, insisting that the entire "old gang" be there to see Saddam Hussein "receive his plaque."

As President Franken demonstrated exactly how he would strangle Saddam Hussein, on a ripe pineapple from one of *Air Force One*'s frequently replenished fruit bowls, an explosion off the left side of the plane marked their passage into Iraqi airspace and convinced Admiral Itzkowitz that perhaps he needed to make further adjustments in the President's medication.

Risking court-martial, the admiral administered a powerful sedative, telling the President it was more Zoloft. As Franken drifted off into a deep sleep, a relieved Ornstein ordered the plane to turn back toward the United States.

13

"MY FELLOW AMERICANS, so much has happened in the past ninety-nine days that I hardly know where to begin. First, let me say that I pledge my complete cooperation and that of my administration with the Joint Congressional Committee on the President's Mood Swings."

It was with mixed emotions that Norman Ornstein watched his president and best friend give the most important speech of his life. On the one hand, Ornstein was relieved that the complex psychoactive chemicals that had played such an unfortunate role in the events of the past three months were now finally purged from the President's system. On the other hand, he was worried that the overwhelmingly popular support for the

President's aborted plan to kill Saddam Hussein personally might one day fade, leaving the administration at the mercy of the jackals in Congress.

Franken himself seemed sobered and calm, a more mature man for having endured the ordeal of his prolonged bipolar episode. And as Franken read the text of the speech Ornstein had written for him, word-for-word for a change, the chief of staff, mindful of the difficult road that lay ahead, dared to hope that the worst was finally behind them.

"The events of the last few months have been confusing and upsetting to many people, including me. All of us are prisoners of our endocrine systems, which like our Social Security system are in desperate need of reform."

Ornstein allowed himself a small smile at his own joke, which he thought was one of the wittiest he'd ever written.

"Perhaps this chart will help clarify exactly what happened to your president and caused me to behave in such an unstable manner. It shows the level of the chemical serotonin in my brain at various times throughout my young administration."

The chart, which Franken had propped up on an easel to the left (his left) of his desk, resembled a schematic for a particularly terrifying roller coaster, the kind that had been rendered obsolete in most states by punitive civil liability actions. Using a state-of-the-art retractable pointer, the President traced the towering peaks and deep, dark valleys of his brain chemistry.

"This low point here begins on the day following my inaugural address and continues to here, where I began a course of drug therapy administered by my former physician, former rear admiral Lawrence Itzkowitz."

The mere mention of the name of the quackish naval psychiatrist sent an involuntary shudder down Ornstein's spine. The chief of staff pitied the sailors of Aegis-class destroyer *Betty Ford*, who would be ministered to by now Lieutenant (j.g.) Itzkowitz.

"My serotonin level continued to rise until this peak here, the day on which I had myself cloned. Then, due to adjustments in my medication, you'll note that my serotonin level plummeted, causing this low point here, which coincides with the unfortunate incident involving President Mandela. After increasing my dosage to three hundred milligrams of Zoloft a day, my serotonin level spiked radically during this period here when I was planning the assassination of President Hussein and taking intensive Spanish lessons."

Noting the approach of a low pressure system outside the window over the President's left shoulder, Dick Morris nodded approvingly at Franken's virtuoso performance. It seemed to him that the President's delivery struck precisely the right balance between courage and sorrow, forcefulness and humility, hope for the future and regret for the past, and a certain older but wiser *je ne sais quoi* and an indefinable more-in-sadness-than-in-anger miffedness at the lamentable malpractice he had endured.

The other members of the Five Wise Men—Steingarten, Kleinbaum, Ornstein, and Fineman—shared Morris's appreciation for the masterful exhibition of sheer political bravura. And as one, they breathed a collective sigh of relief, tempered in Kleinbaum's case by a small amount of acid reflux caused by a stress-related weakening of his pyloric sphincter. But what happened next would tax even the strongest sphincters in the room.

The President reached into his desk and pulled out a battered notebook, which Kleinbaum, to his horror, recognized instantly. Opening the book to an earmarked page, Franken began to read.

"March 11th. Suicidal feelings stronger than ever. But I know I must continue to struggle against despair for the sake of my family and for the good of the nation. Millions are counting on me to do what is right, and I must continue to live and find a way to endure this devastating emotional torture. And though they will never know the superhuman struggle

I have waged against the irresistible desire to end it all, I must persevere against self-pity, alone, in this dank prison called the presidency, watched over by my ungrateful jailers, the American people. Perhaps if I took the Zoloft before meals on an empty sto—and so on and so forth." Franken closed the book and paused.

"He didn't just do that?" Ornstein asked Fineman.

"No, he didn't," Fineman answered. "Because if he did, he'd be crazy. And he just told us he's not crazy anymore, right?"

Steingarten's face was frozen in a rictus of fear.

"Peter, you can always go back to the American Enterprise Institute," Morris joked hollowly.

"Dick, I could no more go back to AEI than you could get another two-and-a-half-million-dollar book advance," Steingarten jibed in response.

"No! Noooooooo!" Joel Kleinbaum had begun to wail.

"Joel, sssshh, they'll hear you on television," Norm Ornstein whispered urgently.

"Noooooooooo!!!!"

If the President could hear Kleinbaum moaning and then retching into a wastebasket, he gave no sign.

"That is an entry from the diary in which I have recorded my innermost thoughts every day of my adult life except for a couple of years ago when I took a four-week vacation in the Bahamas. I don't need to tell you that those words were written in a very dark moment. The words speak for themselves. That's what words do. And now, whenever I start to feel like I'm losing control, I open my diary and read that entry, or one of the many just like it, to remind myself how low a man can sink and just how far I have risen. I guarantee that, as your president, I will not allow myself to feel helpless and unloved ever again. And I will never allow my America, our America, to feel helpless and unloved either! Thank you. God bless you. Keep a diary, it really helps."

Otto Franken and Dan Haggerty burst into the Oval Office.

"Great speech, Al!" Otto said, embracing his brother.

Haggerty, in turn, wrapped them both in an enormous bear hug, ignoring the cameras that were still rolling a few feet away.

14

"WE COULD JUST DESTROY THE DIARIES," President Franken suggested, "but that would be wrong."

"Joel, is there anything in the specific language of the Congressional Committee's subpoena that we could use to justify withholding the sensitive entries?" Peter Steingarten asked.

"All the entries are sensitive, dipshit!" Joel Kleinbaum's temper flared. "Either he's pissing on the people of New Hampshire and Iowa, balling some hooker, or taking a payoff from one of your insurance buddies."

"That's not fair!" the President objected. "And if you're going to get into that kind of detail, maybe we should ask Bob Woodward to step out of the room for a while."

Woodward, whose book was due in less than two hours, was only too eager to leave the room.

THE END

*TRANSCRIPT OF NORMAN J. ORNSTEIN'S TESTIMONY
BEFORE THE JOINT CONGRESSIONAL COMMITTEE TO
INVESTIGATE THE PRESIDENT'S MOOD SWINGS*

Senator Orrin Hatch (R-Utah)
and Representative Dennis Looney (D-Mass.)
Chairmen

SENATOR HATCH: First of all, Mr. Ornstein, welcome.
We appreciate your appearance before our committee
in response to our subpoenas and the subsequent
court order.

NORMAN ORNSTEIN: Mr. Chairman, I'm sorry I couldn't
have appeared before the committee sooner, but as
you know, my counsel advised me to . . . well, you
know. And I hope you didn't take our many attempts
to quash your subpoenas personally.

SEN. HATCH: Not at all. And I, in turn, hope you
did not resent being served with the court order
during your daughter's birthday party by a man
dressed as a circus ringmaster leading a troupe
of trained dogs.

MR. ORNSTEIN: Hardly. My daughter thought they
were terrific. She's at that age where she loves
anything having to do with animals. Now, with
your permission, Mr. Chairman, I'd like to make
an opening statement.

SEN. HATCH: All right, Mr. Ornstein. But it had
better be relevant to the matter at hand. And I
give you fair warning: If at any time I decide
that you are flouting the authority of this
committee, the sergeant-at-arms is present and is
prepared to bind and gag you as he did Attorney
General Kleinbaum.

MR. ORNSTEIN: Fair enough. I'll read my statement then. "Almost twenty years ago, the world was stunned by the discovery of dozens of diaries allegedly written by Adolf Hitler. These diaries were authenticated by the most distinguished experts in the fields of graphology and document verification and were not revealed to be fakes until weeks later when experts from the Bic company discovered quite by accident that the diaries had been written with a ballpoint pen. There was a rush to judgment then, and there has been a rush to judgment now. Twenty years ago people of good will, not just graphologists and document verifiers, vowed, 'Never again!' Never again would there be a rush to judgment based on diaries of dubious origin."

SEN. HATCH: Let me get this straight, Mr. Ornstein. Are you saying the President's diaries are a forgery?

MR. ORNSTEIN: I'm saying that the *Hitler* diaries were a forgery, and there was a rush to judgment.

SEN. HATCH: I see. Sergeant-at-arms!

REP. LOONEY: Just a moment, Senator Hatch, if I may. I'd like to hear the rest of Mr. Ornstein's testimony instead of just having him nod or shake his head with a gag in his mouth the way the attorney general did.

SEN. HATCH: All right. But Mr. Ornstein, I'm warning you: Any further attempt to distract us with meaningless comparisons between the evidence before the committee and the Hitler diaries will be met with the most severe sanction.

MR. ORNSTEIN: Uh, okay, sorry.

SEN. HATCH: We'll begin the questioning with Representative Mary Bono.

REP. MARY BONO (R—CA.): Mr. Ornstein, what is your exact job title?

MR. ORNSTEIN: I'm chief of staff to the President of the United States.

REP. BONO: And what exactly is the nature of your duties? Were you elected to this position?

SEN. HATCH: Maybe we'd better start with someone else. Senator Biden?

SENATOR JOSEPH BIDEN (D—DEL.): Mr. Ornstein, thank you for taking the time out of what I know what must be a very busy schedule dealing with the dozens of civil actions that are being taken against you and the President. It can't be fun.

MR. ORNSTEIN: You can say that again, Senator.

SEN. BIDEN: You know, this isn't fun for us either. It isn't a fun subject. All of us suffer at one time or another from incapacitating mood swings. And the members of this, the Looney-Hatch Committee, which by the way, strikes me as a pretty appropos name, are no exception. Mental instability is an unfortunate fact of life here on Capitol Hill, often interfering with the conduct of government, and even leading to its shutdown on two occasions in 1995. Still, the President has a special obligation to exercise restraint and self-control during periods of unavoidable emotional distress. Mr. Ornstein, did you ever see the President weeping?

MR. ORNSTEIN: The President did weep at

Henry Kissinger's eightieth birthday party
when Celine Dion sang "My Heart Will Go On."

SEN. BIDEN: That's completely understandable.
Even the Vietnamese ambassador was crying.
I meant weeping *for no apparent reason.*

MR. ORNSTEIN: No. Absolutely not.

SEN. BIDEN: That's all the questions I have,
Mr. Chairman.

SEN. HATCH: Thank you, Senator Biden. It's good to
have you remind us of the importance of compassion
and the universality of human frailty. We are all
flawed beings. Congressman Burton, your questions?

REP. DAN BURTON (R—IND.): Mr. Ornstein, are you
familiar with Exhibit RR?

MR. ORNSTEIN: Exhibit RR? Would that be the plaque
inscribed to Saddam Hussein naming him as "the
world's greatest granddad?"

REP. BURTON: No, Mr. Ornstein, that's Exhibit NN.
I'm talking about Double R. The diaries.

MR. ORNSTEIN: Oh yes, I have that in front of me.

REP. BURTON: And have you and your attorney had
an opportunity to examine the diaries?

MR. LOUIS "BUD" BENNETT (ATTORNEY FOR
MR. ORNSTEIN): Yes, we have.

SEN. HATCH: Mr. Bennett, you're not allowed to
answer for your client.

MR. BENNETT: So I'm just supposed to sit here like

a pot plant? I mean, potted plant?

REP. LOONEY: I'm curious. Mr. Bennett, are you related to Bob and Bill Bennett?

MR. BENNETT: Yes, I'm their younger brother. I've been somewhat overshadowed by the two of them and their accomplishments, but I can assure I'm every bit as smart and wily as they are.

SEN. HATCH: Clearly. But please, if you'd follow the rules here and not simply call out the answers for your client.

MR. BENNETT: Right. Okay.

SEN. HATCH: Mr. Burton?

REP. BURTON: Mr. Ornstein, with reference to Exhibit RR, the diaries, could you tell us please who the President is referring to when he uses the letters "O," "N," and "P"?

MR. ORNSTEIN: I cannot say for sure, Senator.

REP. BURTON: Isn't it true that you are "N"?

MR. ORNSTEIN: I don't know for certain. I guess you'd have to ask the President.

REP. BURTON: Well, we'd like to ask the President, but we understand that you have advised him not to answer any of our questions and to claim executive privilege.

MR. ORNSTEIN: Is that a question, Mr. Burton?

REP. BURTON: Okay, you want a question?! I'll give

you a question! Did you advise the President not to answer our questions?

MR. ORNSTEIN: Any advice I might have given the President would have been in response to a question that he asked me and equally subject to executive privilege as any answers to any questions that you might have asked him.

REP. BURTON: Okay, if want to play that game, fine. Let's try another approach. Mr. Ornstein have you ever had occasion to dial 1-900-FRANKEN or 1-900-LESBIAN?

MR. ORNSTEIN: Not that I can recall.

REP. BURTON: Mr. Ornstein, you are under oath, sir!

MR. BENNETT: We know that!

MR. ORNSTEIN: Bud, please.

REP. BURTON: Mr. Ornstein would it surprise you to learn that both 1-900-FRANKEN and 1-900-LESBIAN connect to an Iowa-based phone sex business owned by one "Dotto Dranken"?

MR. BENNETT: Have you no decency, sir?!

MR. ORNSTEIN: Bud, c'mon.

REP. BURTON: Mr. Ornstein, I am waiting for an answer. And I am prepared to wait until hell freezes over!

MR. ORNSTEIN: Mr. Burton, I have read over exhibit AAA, which are the documents appearing to suggest that a Dotto Dranken of Muscatine, Iowa, did in fact own the phone sex business you mentioned.

MR. BURTON: So . . . that's a "yes"?

MR. ORNSTEIN: Yes.

SEN. HATCH: Who wants to go next? Ted?

SENATOR TED KENNEDY (D—MASS.): Mr. Ornstein, would you say that you have a difficult job?

MR. ORNSTEIN: Well, it is an honor to serve the President and my country, and while my job is at times very challenging, it has its rewards and is certainly no more difficult than the jobs that millions of hardworking Americans do without complaint every day, such as being a janitor in a mental health facility or, I don't know, prepping diseased dogs for surgery.

SEN. KENNEDY: That would require shaving the dogs?

MR. ORNSTEIN: Yes.

SEN. KENNEDY: And shaving the diseased dogs in preparation for surgery, that is a minimum-wage job, is it not?

MR. ORNSTEIN: Yes, it is.

SEN. KENNEDY: And President Franken is in favor of raising the minimum wage?

MR. ORNSTEIN: Yes.

SEN. KENNEDY: Thank you, Mr. Ornstein. And good luck to you, sir. But if you'll excuse me, I have to appear at a bond hearing for one of my nephews.

SEN. HATCH: Thank you, Ted. Senator Smith.

SEN. ROBERT SMITH (R—N.H.): Mr. Ornstein, I want to get back to the diaries. The President refers to the residents of my state as "brain-dead mouth breathers," "slack-jawed morons," and "candidates for Dr. Kevorkian's shortlist." Now, since I am a New Hampshire native myself, maybe I'm too stupid to understand what the President meant. So perhaps you could clarify the President's comments. Because I am sure my constituents in New Hampshire would like to know how the President feels about them.

MR. ORNSTEIN: Senator, I'm a political scientist, not a linguist or semanticist or semiotician. I am not an expert on words or their meanings.

SENATOR STROM THURMOND (R—S.C.): With respect, Mr. Ornstein, that is possibly the worst evasion of a question I have ever encountered in my fifty-three years in the senate.

MR. ORNSTEIN: You're right, Senator Thurmond, I'm sorry. I can only say in respect to expressions cited by Senator Smith and the many other pejorative allusions to the residents of other states in which primaries are held, that in all my private conversations with the President, he has expressed only the greatest respect and admiration for the fine people of New Hampshire or what have you.

SEN. SMITH: Then why would he on page 174 of the exhibit describe the people of my state as "the kind of subhuman mongoloids who prove once and for all that cousins shouldn't marry"?

MR. ORNSTEIN: Uh, Senator, it's important to remember that the President was a comedy writer. And I think what may have been going on there is that after a long, hard day of campaigning, trying to get across a message of hope for the future, that the President may have used the diary-keeping process as a sort of "catharsis," if you will.

SEN. SMITH: A catharsis?

MR. ORNSTEIN: Exactly.

SEN. THURMOND: Senator Smith, if I may. Mr. Ornstein, on page 672, there is reference to the President having sex with two underage cheerleaders who could, and I quote, "suck the chrome off a trailer hitch." Is that the kind of catharsis you're talking about?

MR. ORNSTEIN: Many men, and I suppose women, have vivid fantasy lives, which reflect harmless wish fulfillments, and I suppose that some of these men and women record these fantasies in so-called diaries, as a, well, catharsis.

SEN. SMITH: Mr. Ornstein, does the President have a dark side?

MR. ORNSTEIN: No.

SEN. HATCH: Time has expired, Senator. Mr. Frank?

REP. BARNEY FRANK (D—MASS.): Mr. Ornstein, how are you today, sir?

MR. ORNSTEIN: Well, I'd rather be at home watching myself on C-SPAN. (LAUGHTER)

REP. FRANK: You're actually on all the major networks. And CBS too. (LAUGHTER) Mr. Ornstein, I want to ask you a question that relates more directly to the stated purpose of this committee. Which is: How was the President's mood when you last saw him?

MR. ORNSTEIN: Good. His mood was good. He is

upbeat, and eager to continue the work he was
elected to do.

REP. FRANK: Is he continuing with the Spanish?

MR. ORNSTEIN: Yes. As you know, this country's trade
with the Spanish-speaking countries south of the border pumps more than ninety billion dollars into our
economy each year, and the President hopes use his
new language skills when he visits Brazil next month.

SEN. HATCH: Isn't Brazil Portuguese-speaking?

MR. ORNSTEIN: Yes, the two languages are very
similar.

REP. FRANK: Mr. Ornstein, you mentioned that the
President spent the better part of his career as a
comedy writer.

MR. ORNSTEIN: Yes, that's true.

REP. FRANK: And he was a very talented one
at that. Isn't it true that he wrote the Greek
restaurant bit from the early years of *Saturday
Night Live,* where John Belushi would say
"cheeborgie, cheeborgie, cheeborgie"?

MR. ORNSTEIN: Actually, that was Don Novello.

REP. FRANK: Oh. Well, "The baseball been berry-
berry good to me"? That one?

MR. ORNSTEIN: No. That wasn't him either. That was
Alan Zweibel.

REP. FRANK: Really? Because I thought I had read in
his autobiography that the President had written
that with Simone de Beauvoir.

MR. ORNSTEIN: Nope. Zweibel.

REP. FRANK: Well, nevertheless, you get my point.

MR. ORNSTEIN: Yes. He did write "The Guy with the Unusually Long Nose Hairs."

REP. FRANK: Exactly. And that character had nose hairs that hung all the way down below his waist.

MR. ORNSTEIN: Right.

REP. FRANK: And what was funny about that was that it was so exaggerated. No one has nose hairs that long, do they?

MR. ORNSTEIN: Right, Congressman. It was a flight of fancy, if you will.

REP. FRANK: "Flight of fancy." We'd do well to remember that phrase here today. "Flight of fancy." Is my time up? No? Okay. Um, how about "Roseanne Roseannadanna"? Who wrote that?

MR. ORNSTEIN: That was also Alan Zweibel.

REP. LOONEY: Mr. Frank, your time is up.

SEN. DON NICKLES (R—OK.): Mr. Ornstein, to the best of your knowledge, did the President ever receive campaign contributions from the insurance industry for the purposes of advancing their agenda?

MR. ORNSTEIN: Only to the extent that their agenda is America's agenda, yes. But I'm glad you brought that up, Senator, because I have here in my hand a list of members of this committee who have received campaign contributions from the insurance industry.

Some of the numbers are quite substantial. For example, you, Senator Nickles . . .

SEN. NICKLES: You bastard!

SEN. HATCH: Please, Senator Nickles! Sit down! And
stop waving your arms and spitting . . . thank you.
Senator Santorum?

SENATOR RICK SANTORUM (R—PA.): Mr. Ornstein,
the manufacture and testing of antidepressants is
the second-largest industry in my home state of
Pennsylvania. Did the President consider the damage
he might be doing to the antidepressant industry by
blaming Zoloft for his erratic behavior?

MR. ORNSTEIN: Senator, the President has made
it very clear that his own psychopharmacological
imbalance is unique to him personally and by no
means reflective of the experience of the two-
thirds of all Americans who now take antidepressants daily with no other side effects than
occasional dry mouth, dizziness, or loss of
sexual vitality.

SEN. SANTORUM: I move to have that last statement
about sexual vitality stricken from the record.

REP. LOONEY: Without objection.

SEN. SANTORUM: Thank you. I have no further
questions.

SEN. HATCH: Representative Gore?

REP. AL GORE (I—TENN.): Hi, Mr. Ornstein,
remember me?

MR. ORNSTEIN: Yes, Mr. Vice President.

REP. GORE: It's just "Congressman" now. Plain old Congressman Al Gore.

MR. ORNSTEIN: Nothing wrong with that, Congressman.

REP. GORE: You're damn right, there's nothing wrong with that!

SEN. HATCH: Mr. Gore, sir, if you'd please sit down and stop waving your arms like that. Yes, like that. Stop that.

REP. GORE: Sorry, Mr. Chairman. Before I begin my questioning, I'd like to respond to allegations that have appeared in the press that I bear some sort of personal animus toward President Franken and the men who advised him during his campaign, such as Mr. Ornstein here. Specifically that I bear a grudge for the immoral, dishonest, and as we now know from Mr. Ornstein's own memos, *illegal* tactics that the President's team used against me and my family.

MR. BENNETT: And your crooked buddies in the banking industry.

MR. GORE: You shut up! As I was saying before I was so rudely interrupted, what Franken did to me was utterly loathsome. Nonetheless, I have put that behind me, and I am not at all bitter about the dashing of my lifelong ambitions. Indeed, I am grateful for the opportunity to serve my country as a freshman congressman from the sixth district of Tennessee and to be the ranking member of the special subcommittee on Marine Salvage Rights in Intercoastal Waterways.

MR. ORNSTEIN: The President and Interior Secretary

Ralph Lauren have been following the work of your sub-committee very closely, Mr. Vice Pre—uh, Congressman, and they think you guys have come up with some terrific stuff.

REP. GORE: Yeah, right. Mr. Ornstein, I'm going to make this very simple. There is an exhibit, which I believe is labeled Triple I, which consists of a memo you wrote to the President on August 11th, 1999.

MR. ORNSTEIN: Which memo is that, Congressman?

REP. GORE: It's the one titled: "Capitalizing on Our Recent Success" and marked, quote, "Secret: Please Destroy After Reading."

MR. BENNETT: Don't answer that.

MR. ORNSTEIN: Bud, it's okay.

REP. GORE: Now this memo was among the documents Scotch-taped into the President's diary along with some Polaroids of a Ms. Terri Barnstable of North Cutely, New Hampshire. You remember those Polaroids? You're in some of them.

MR. ORNSTEIN: Yes, I am familiar with the Polaroids. Both from the evidentiary material and from their publication in *Penthouse* magazine. By the way, did you know that the Polaroid Company employs more than seven thousand people in the Boston area, including hundreds of underprivileged youths to whom they offer job training?

REP. GORE: Yes. I'm sure if Senator Kennedy were here instead of at the office of the Kennedy family bail bondsman, he would have pointed that out himself and saved you the trouble. But I don't really

give a shit about jobs and underprivileged kids.
Wait a minute. Scratch that. What I meant to say is
that jobs and underprivileged kids are irrelevant
to the matter at hand.

MR. ORNSTEIN: With all due respect, Congressman
Gore, as far as this administration is concerned,
jobs and underprivileged kids are very relevant.
Now, if the committee has no further
questions . . .

SEN. HATCH: Sit down, Mr. Ornstein.

REP. GORE: Look, Ornstein. We can do this fast. Or
we can do this slow. It's up to you.

MR. ORNSTEIN: Fast. Let's do it fast.

REP. GORE: Yes. Let's. Mr. Ornstein, in this document, your secret memo to Al Franken, you refer to
"possibly illegal activities." Do you believe that
the activities listed in that part of the memo are
possibly illegal?

MR. ORNSTEIN: At that time, yes.

REP. GORE: Good. Now we're getting somewhere. Moving on. In the part of the memo in which you refer
to "illegal activities," do you believe that the
activities listed there are illegal?

MR. ORNSTEIN: Again, Congressman, at that point
in time—

REP. GORE: And in the part of the memo in which you
refer to "very illegal activities," do you believe
that those activities are, in fact, very illegal?

MR. ORNSTEIN: Illegal, yes. Whether or not they're

very illegal is really a subjective judgment upon which reasonable men may differ.

REP. GORE: And finally, Mr. Ornstein, do you think that a person or persons who commit activities that are "possibly illegal," "illegal," and "very illegal" should be punished in accordance with the laws of the United States of America no matter who that person or persons happen to be?

MR. BENNETT: Whoa. Now, hold on . . .

REP. GORE: Yes, Mr. Bennett?

MR. BENNETT: Uh . . . objection?

REP. GORE: No.

MR. BENNETT: Well, no further questions then.

REP. LOONEY: Nice try, Mr. Bennett, but Rep. Gore still has several more minutes of his allotted time remaining.

REP. GORE: Mr. Chairman, if I may, I'd like to use the balance of my time to take a good hard look at Mr. Ornstein to try and get some iota of understanding of what kind of man could do the things that he has done.

(SEVERAL MINUTES OF STARING)

SEN. HATCH: Okay. Time's up. Thank you, Mr. Ornstein. We'll see you after lunch, hopefully without Mr. Bennett. One last thing. Mr. Ornstein, I hope I don't need to order you locked up during lunch to ensure that you don't do anything stupid like flee the country.

MR. BENNETT: Mr. Chairman, my client is a respected professional with deep roots in the community.

SEN. HATCH: Right. That's what I thought. Sergeant-at-arms! Lock him up.

TRANSCRIPT OF ADDRESS BY
PRESIDENT AL FRANKEN TO THE NATION

JUNE 10, 2001 2:45 A.M. E.D.T.

My fellow Americans. Good morning, except on
the West Coast. To those of you out there, good
evening. I apologize for speaking to you at such
a late hour, but it was just minutes ago that my
advisors, as well as my family and Ambassador-
designate Haggerty, finally persuaded me that
it is in the best interest of the nation that
I resign the office of the presidency.

My letter of resignation was drafted with the
gracious assistance of Chief Justice William
Rehnquist, so you can bet it's legal, and was
hand-delivered to Vice President Lieberman,
or President Lieberman, as I guess I should
call him now.

Hopefully, this will bring to an end the turmoil,
as well as to the numerous legal actions pending
against me and my staff, occasioned by the politically motivated disclosure of the contents of my
private diaries.

Let me say here and now that I regret very deeply
the harm that I've done both to people I care about
and people I don't really care about all that much.
I am sorry. I apologize. It was wrong. What I did
was wrong. I'm sorry. I am so, so sorry. Boy, am
I sorry.

To the people of New Hampshire, who really took it
on the chin in my diaries, I feel terrible. Your
state is not by any means a "shithole," and all I
can say is that someday I hope you will find it in

your hearts to welcome me and my family back to Lake Hugabug, where my kids learned to canoe.

To the people of Iowa, whom I described as perhaps not the cleverest or most attractive citizens of our great country, please let me say that I was wrong about you. In order to make amends, as my last official act I have signed an executive order purchasing 30 million tons of soybeans, which will be sent to Russia to try to help them deal with the ridiculous mess over there. I hope that that will square things between me and Iowa.

In the last several weeks, much has been made of my use of the shorthand phrase "S.P.," both in my diaries and in the transcripts from the Oval Office taping system. Well, let me just say this: If anyone is "S" it is me. Not you, the "P."

Of all the inappropriate conduct I am ashamed of, I am most ashamed of the inappropriate conduct I engaged in during my campaign with women who were not my wife. In conducting these relationships with these women who were not my wife, I misled people, even my wife. This matter is now between me, my wife, our daughter, and, to a lesser extent, our son. I must make it right. We must have time to heal. Therefore, at noon tomorrow, we will be leaving on United Flight 211 for Honolulu and a three-week stay at the home of comedienne Ellen DeGeneres and her life partner, Anne Heche, who recently had my clone implanted in her uterus. But that's a topic for another speech.

While I take full responsibility for the misfortunes that have befallen my presidency, others are not entirely without blame. It had been my intention to pardon members of my staff and my administration. But

I forgot. Sorry. I must now leave it up to the good graces of President Lieberman to do so.

I did, however, manage, with the reluctant assistance of Chief Justice Rehnquist, to pardon myself. This will enable me to retain the prerogatives of an ex-president, including my pension, an office and staff at taxpayer expense, lifelong Secret Service protection, and, eventually, burial in Arlington National Cemetery beneath an eternal flame.

It is my fondest wish that, in the fullness of time, the American people will look back on the Franken presidency as something of a mixed bag and not as a complete disaster.

And so I now leave the great national stage, upon which I have tried to tread with dignity. If I have on occasion fallen short, it was not due to a lack of faith in the American people, oh, no, but merely the result of a chemical imbalance in that great mystery we call "the brain."

This is my problem. Not yours.

Thank you. May God bless you. I'm sorry.

PART FOUR

EPILOGUE

Hello, and welcome

to the Al Franken Presidential Library here in Hartford, Connecticut.

I am your interactive holographic tour guide. You might be thinking

that I look a lot like President Al Franken. There's a good reason for

that. My name is Professor Alonzo Heche-DeGeneres. I was cloned in the year 2001, from some of Al Franken's cheek cells during one of

the manic episodes he suffered while president. I was raised by my

birth mother, Anne Heche, and her life partner, Ellen DeGeneres,

whom I consider my father. I tell you this because many people are

unfamiliar with the process of human cloning, which was outlawed

by President Joseph Lieberman on the day he took office.

Before we begin, a word about my qualifications to be your tour

guide. I am the author of seven books and four CD-ROMs on the life

and times of President Al Franken, as well as a book on human cloning.

Some people think when they first meet me and hear my story that I

am obsessed with President Franken because I am his clone. Not at all.

In fact, for many years my mother, Anne, and my father, Ellen, shielded

me from the knowledge that I was the first and only human clone in

history and that the disgraced former president was my genetic fore-

bear. As homosexuals, my parents place undue stock in the concept

that our genes determine our destiny, a view that I now reject categori-

cally. As such, they kept me isolated from all contact with the outside

world in their geodesic dome on the island of Kauai in Hawaii, the only

state in which their marriage was considered legal.

I first noticed my uncanny resemblance to former president

Franken while watching President Lieberman's funeral on my video

wall on Kauai. There, standing at the gravesite of the towering figure now considered to be one of our nation's greatest presidents, was a man who, though fifty years older than I, could in all other respects have been my identical twin.

After querying my parents' best friend, k. d. lang, who has always been a straight shooter in my book, I discovered the secret of my origin and set out across the country in search of Al Franken, a man whom, at that time, I considered to be every bit as much my father as Ellen DeGeneres.

I tracked him down living in a large, comfortable house in the Philadelphia district of New York City. I followed him for several days, gathering my courage for what I hoped would be a warm and joyful reunion. However, just as I was approaching him at a franchise of the McDonald's Fruit Smoothie chain, I saw him embrace a young woman, whom I assumed to be his daughter but now believe to have been a prostitute.

It was a defining moment. I declared my independence from Al Franken, with whom I share nothing except my DNA, and decided to go my own way. I have never looked back, except in the normal course of my studies of the Franken era during the writing of my Ph.D. thesis, my books, and my CD-ROMs. Also, I teach a course on the Franken presidency as part of my duties as Ralph Lauren Professor of Modern American History at the University of Wyoming, Cheyenne.

But enough about me.

If you'll follow me through the atrium, we will begin our tour. The room you are standing in features one hundred and forty-four equally spaced sculpture alcoves, each containing a bust of Al Franken by a different artist. These one hundred and forty-four sculpture alcoves symbolize the one hundred and forty-four days of the Franken presidency.

Now, some may ask, "Why build a presidential library to honor a president who was only in office for one hundred and forty-four days before being impeached and arrested?" The answer is simple. The library is here so that posterity can learn from the Franken presidency with all of its failures, and, yes, successes.

I hear some of you chuckling. See? That's right. I *am* fully interactive and, yes, I hear you chuckling. But despite the preconceptions that many of you may hold, the Franken presidency was not without its successes. For example, the complete and final dismantling of the anticompetitive Glass-Steagle Act paved the way for the total domination of the financial services industry by giant insurance conglomerates that we enjoy today. The selection of Joseph Lieberman as the President's running-mate and, therefore, successor made possible the nineteen-year-long Golden Era of the Lieberman Administration.

The federally mandated inclusion of water-soluble bonding agents in chewing gum, an idea which President Franken conceived and executed during one of his manic highs, virtually eliminated unsightly gum stains from our cities' sidewalks. Finally, the expansion of NATO to include the Russian Federation, while controversial at the time, has proven to be a bulwark of stability in a changing world.

After you pass through this hallway, which showcases the plaque proclaiming Saddam Hussein to be "the world's greatest granddad," you'll come to this replica of the Oval Office, which has been built at one hundred and forty-four percent of life size.

The display features wax figures of the President and his Inner Circle. The man who looks exactly like me, sitting behind the desk in his bathrobe, is President Franken. The man injecting the President with a stimulant is Rear Admiral Lawrence Itzkowitz, who later won the Navy Cross for his heroic efforts during the Third Persian Gulf War, when he helped the captain of the Aegis-class destroyer *Betty Ford* keep his shit together during the height of battle. Here's an interesting side note: During the time of the Franken presidency, the word *shit* was considered offensive.

The man standing to the left of the President (his left) is chief of staff Norman Ornstein, later Sri Bhagwan Muktananda, who served two and a half years at the minimum security prison at Allenwood, Pennsylvania, for his role in the scandals surrounding the President's administration.

The man restraining the President's brother Otto is treasury secretary Peter Steingarten, who spent eighteen months at Allenwood, working first in the laundry and then as the prison tennis pro.

Press Secretary Howard Fineman, shown speaking on the phone to Sharif Parvez, an Iranian-born Jaguar mechanic, served less than a year in Allenwood and later became a Daimler-Chrysler Award–winning columnist for *Road & Track* magazine.

The man holding his head in his right hand and reaching for an antacid with his left is Attorney General Joel Kleinbaum. It was his incompetence in failing to keep the President's diaries out of the hands of his enemies in Congress that led directly to Franken's downfall. Joel Kleinbaum served less than a week of his nine-year sentence at Allenwood before being killed by an errant golf ball driven by former Disney chairman Michael Eisner, who had been imprisoned following the Space Mountain disaster of 2002.

The man shown whispering to reporter Bob Woodward is the President's political consultant Dick Morris, who escaped jail time when he agreed to testify against the President and his advisors.

He received a five-million-dollar advance for his book about the downfall of the Franken presidency, *The Annotated Franken Diaries,* which was a major commercial failure and led to a general disinterest in books of any sort.

The President's brother, Otto Franken, you all know. His Internet sex and gambling empire has made him the world's richest person.

The man dozing on the couch is Ambassador Dan Haggerty, whose acting career never got the shot in the arm he hoped it would from his appointment as ambassador to Great Britain. However, his friend Otto Franken remained loyal until the end, personally financing a string of money-losing Grizzly Adams movies, including *Grizzly Adams's Caribbean Vacation, Grizzly Adams Down Under,* and *Escape from Grizzly Adams.*

This re-creation of the Oval Office is accurate down to the last detail, including the Chinese food containers spread throughout the room, the unpacked boxes stacked in front of the fire exit, and the presence of First Lady Franni Franken, who is shown vacuuming.

Now please follow me down this poorly illuminated staircase, which symbolizes the dark days following the President's impeachment. The two hundred and forty-four steps represent the one hundred and forty-four days the President served in office plus the one hundred United States senators who voted to convict the President. Oooop! Watch yourself there, miss. See? Fully interactive. Okay, a few more steps to go. Just a few more. Aaaand . . . we're here.

Here deep below the Presidential Library you can see the geothermal-power-generating system that makes the library so very expensive to operate. The geothermal system was installed after one of the solar panels on the roof fell and injured a visiting Gay Scout.

Shall we take the elevator back up? Good. This enormous and brightly lit elevator, named in memory of the President's friend and mentor, Reverend Thaddeus Thorndike, represents the redemptive power of Almighty God to lift even the most miserable of us sinners to everlasting glory. If you look above you on the wall to my left, you'll see the words "judge not," and on the wall to the right, the words "lest ye be judged." President Franken always felt it was important that we judge not lest we in turn be judged. At least after his impeachment, he felt that way.

Now stepping out here, you'll see twelve dioramas representing each of the twelve pitch meetings that President Franken attended after being released from Allenwood, attempting to sell his television drama *Helicopter Rescue Squad.*

Again suffering from depression after the failure of *Helicopter Rescue Squad,* President Franken descended into what was without question the darkest period in his life, represented by this long, dark tube that we must crawl through on our hands and knees. Watch your head, please, sir. President Franken would later say that on a scale of depression, being impeached and jailed was a "three," while the cancellation of *Helicopter Rescue Squad* was a "ten-plus."

Squeezing now through the extremely narrow opening at the end of the dark tube, we enter the final destination on our tour, the Hall of Salvation. The ceiling of this vast room is more than one hundred and forty-four feet high. Can anyone tell me why I mentioned the figure one hundred and forty-four? Yes, you, young man. No, it's not twelve feet for each of the twelve pitch meetings. Yes, you. Right. One hundred and forty-four days in office.

And can anyone tell me why the architect decided to make the ceiling *higher* than one hundred and forty-four feet? No one? It's *higher* than one hundred and forty-four feet because this is the Hall of *Salvation.* And the gap between one hundred and forty-four and the actual height of the ceiling, one hundred and sixty-three feet, symbolizes the path to salvation.

And indeed Al Franken did find the salvation he so richly deserved. For Al Franken, salvation took the form of the consuming passion of his later years: biblical archaeology. Financed by his brother Otto and aided by remarkable new satellite technology, the

President made one hundred and forty-four digs in the deserts of the Holy Land, discovering among other artifacts the complete skeleton of Jesus Christ still nailed to the cross.

Any questions? Uh-huh. I get that one a lot. Yes, we would like to display Jesus' skeleton at some future point. It's merely a matter of designing and building an exhibition space that does not detract or interfere or impinge on the architectural whole of the museum as it now stands with its one hundred and forty-four sides. As soon as those aesthetic concerns can be satisfied, we do plan to put Jesus on display. Until then He's very comfortable in a box down in our basement near the geothermal power station.

You know, if it were up to me, I'd take one of those bones and clone Jesus. I'm kidding, of course. Human cloning is a crime and also impossible to do from tissue that is no longer living. Also, speaking from personal experience, I can tell you that any clone of Jesus Christ would have *a lot* of issues.

Now, if there are no further questions . . . Oh, sorry. Yes? Yes, the President is still alive and sexually vigorous at age ninety-five. Oh, that wasn't your question? Oh, yes, yes. Actually he visits the museum quite frequently. He's often out in the garden sitting on a bench next to the topiary statue of an enormous Zoloft capsule with his old friend Sri Bhagwan Muktananda. Although the President still refuses to see me or acknowledge my existence, I am told that he and his former chief of staff like to discuss old times as well as the need to lower ATM fees.

Thank you, everyone. You've been a great tour group. A little reminder. The museum will be closing one hundred and forty-four minutes early today to allow for a long overdue cleaning of the depression tube. The complete set of video chips of *Helicopter Rescue Squad* is available in the gift shop along with most of my books and small pieces of Jesus' skeleton.

ACKNOWLEDGMENTS

Thanks especially to my friend Norm Ornstein, who is not just the funniest policy wonk I know but also one of the seven hundred funniest people I know. Also, to Howard Fineman, who came up with ATM fees as my issue, and, therefore, my entire platform.

Leslie Schnur, my editor, who nudged me along, and I mean "noodged." Jonathon Lazear, my agent, who handled Leslie when she noodged too hard.

Jonathon's wife, Wendy, was one of my "readers": people I trust to tell me when I'm right and Leslie is wrong, which happens all the time. Included in this elite group were Norm, Howard, Amy Nathan, Mandy Grunwald, Hazel Lichterman, Loen Kelley, Lawrence O'Donnell Jr., Frank Luntz, David Mandel, and Geoff Rodkey, my old research assistant, who is both very much alive and very funny.

My newer assistant, Jessica Banks, who is now my old assistant, because she's getting her doctorate at M.I.T. (I employ very smart people.) Such as my newest assistant, Robin Epstein.

Thanks to Diane Bartoli, who coordinated the production of the physical book. And to Paul D'Innocenzo, who took the interior photos, and Brian Mulligan, who oversaw the interior design. And Phil Rose, who art directed the jacket, and Adam Weiss, who took the cover photo. Thanks to Dick Morris, who agreed to have his picture taken even though he was not terribly happy with his portrayal in the actual text. And Kristin Cauthorn, Leslie's assistant, who assisted me an awful lot.

To John Markus, my *Lateline* partner, who steered me away from my first bad idea for this book and who is teaching me how to do a sitcom.

And finally, to my wife and kids: I'm sorry.

ABOUT THE AUTHOR

AL FRANKEN is the author of *I'm Good Enough, I'm Smart Enough, and Doggone It, People Like Me!* and *Rush Limbaugh Is a Big Fat Idiot.* He lives in New York City with his wife and two children.